OPPOSING
VIEWPOINTS®
SERIES

| Gendercide

Other Books of Related Interest:

Opposing Viewpoints Series
Anti-Semitism
Human Rights
Sexual Violence
War

At Issue Series
Are Women Paid Fairly?
Child Pornography

Current Controversies Series
Human Trafficking

"Congress shall make no law . . . abridging the freedom of speech, or of the press."

First Amendment to the US Constitution

The basic foundation of our democracy is the First Amendment guarantee of freedom of expression. The Opposing Viewpoints Series is dedicated to the concept of this basic freedom and the idea that it is more important to practice it than to enshrine it.

OPPOSING VIEWPOINTS® SERIES

| Gendercide

Noah Berlatsky, Book Editor

GREENHAVEN PRESS
A part of Gale, Cengage Learning

GALE
CENGAGE Learning·

Farmington Hills, Mich • San Francisco • New York • Waterville, Maine
Meriden, Conn • Mason, Ohio • Chicago

Elizabeth Des Chenes, *Director, Content Strategy*
Cynthia Sanner, *Publisher*
Douglas Dentino, *Manager, New Product*

For more information, contact:
Greenhaven Press
27500 Drake Rd.
Farmington Hills, MI 48331-3535
Or you can visit our Internet site at gale.cengage.com

For product information and technology assistance, contact us at

Gale Customer Support, 1-800-877-4253
For permission to use material from this text or product, submit all requests online at
www.cengage.com/permissions

Further permissions questions can be emailed to permissionrequest@cengage.com

Articles in Greenhaven Press anthologies are often edited for length to meet page requirements. In addition, original titles of these works are changed to clearly present the main thesis and to explicitly indicate the author's opinion. Every effort is made to ensure that Greenhaven Press accurately reflects the original intent of the authors. Every effort has been made to trace the owners of copyrighted material.

Cover image © nando_piezzi/Demotix/Corbis.

LIBRARY OF CONGRESS CATALOGING-IN-PUBLICATION DATA

Gendercide / Noah Berlatsky, book editor.
    pages cm. -- (Opposing viewpoints)
    Includes bibliographical references and index.
    ISBN 978-0-7377-7004-9 (hardcover) -- ISBN 978-0-7377-7005-6 (pbk.)
    1. Sexism. 2. Sex role. 3. Sex preselection. 4. Sex of children, Parental preferences for. 5. Women--Social conditions. 6. Women--Crimes against. 7. Genocide. I. Berlatsky, Noah.
    HQ1237.G44 2014
    305.3--dc23
                                                    2013049624

Printed in the United States of America
1 2 3 4 5 6 7 18 17 16 15 14

Contents

Why Consider Opposing Viewpoints? 11

Introduction 14

Chapter 1: What Are Common Practices of Gendercide in Developing Countries?

Chapter Preface 18

1. Sex-Selective Abortion Is 20
   Leading to Unprecedented Gendercide
   in the Developing World
   The Economist

2. Sex Selection in the Developing World Today 26
   Is Neither Unprecedented nor Gendercide
   Edgar Dahl

3. China's One-Child Policy Has Contributed 32
   to the Abortion of Girls
   Anu Liisanantti and Karin Beese

4. Abortion of Girls Is a Problem in India 42
   Gursharan Singh Kainth

5. Gendercide of Girls in China Has Driven 50
   the Growth of Sex Trafficking
   Susan Tiefenbrun and Christie J. Edwards

6. Worldwide Human Trafficking Is a Myth 57
   Zbigniew Dumienski

Periodical and Internet Sources Bibliography 71

Chapter 2: What Are Common Practices of Gendercide in Developed Countries?

Chapter Preface 73

1. British Immigrant Communities Commit 75
   Gendercide via Sex-Selective Abortion
   Kishwar Desai

2. Stoking Fears That British Immigrant   84
   Communities Commit Gendercide Is Only
   Aimed at Limiting Abortion
   Jennie Bristow

3. Sex-Selective Abortion Must Be Banned in the   92
   United States to Prevent Gendercide of Girls
   Keith Fournier

4. Banning Sex-Selective Abortion   98
   in the United States Will Only Increase
   Sexism and the Gendercide of Girls
   Michelle Goldberg

5. Selective Abortions Prompt Call   104
   for Later Ultrasounds
   Huffington Post

6. Restricting Ultrasound Information in Canada Is   108
   Morally Wrong and Will Not Prevent Gendercide
   Heather Mallick

Periodical and Internet Sources Bibliography   112

Chapter 3: What Is the Relationship Between Gender-Related Violence and Genocide?

Chapter Preface   114

1. Gendercide Is Closely Related to Genocide   116
   Heather McRobie

2. Gendercide Is Genocide   122
   Rita Banerji

3. Mass Rape of Women Can Be a Form   127
   of Genocide
   Anthony Marino

4. Rape of Men Is Often Unacknowledged   142
   During Genocide
   Will Storr

5. Violence Against Women Was an Important   152
   Part of the Holocaust
   Rochelle Saidel

Periodical and Internet Sources Bibliography   156

Chapter 4: Who Is the Target of Gendercide?

Chapter Preface   158

1. Islamic Culture Targets Women for Gendercide   160
   Alexander Christie-Miller

2. Honor Killings of Muslim Males in the West   167
   Daniel Pipes

3. Blood Feuds Are Gendercide Against Men   172
   in the Balkans
   Adam Jones

4. Women Are Targeted for Violence in War   180
   Sandra I. Cheldelin

5. Men Are Disproportionally Targeted for   194
   Violence and Gendercide
   David Benatar

Periodical and Internet Sources Bibliography   199

For Further Discussion   200

Organizations to Contact   202

Bibliography of Books   207

Index   210

Why Consider Opposing Viewpoints?

> *"The only way in which a human being can make some approach to knowing the whole of a subject is by hearing what can be said about it by persons of every variety of opinion and studying all modes in which it can be looked at by every character of mind. No wise man ever acquired his wisdom in any mode but this."*
>
> *John Stuart Mill*

In our media-intensive culture it is not difficult to find differing opinions. Thousands of newspapers and magazines and dozens of radio and television talk shows resound with differing points of view. The difficulty lies in deciding which opinion to agree with and which "experts" seem the most credible. The more inundated we become with differing opinions and claims, the more essential it is to hone critical reading and thinking skills to evaluate these ideas. Opposing Viewpoints books address this problem directly by presenting stimulating debates that can be used to enhance and teach these skills. The varied opinions contained in each book examine many different aspects of a single issue. While examining these conveniently edited opposing views, readers can develop critical thinking skills such as the ability to compare and contrast authors' credibility, facts, argumentation styles, use of persuasive techniques, and other stylistic tools. In short, the Opposing Viewpoints Series is an ideal way to attain the higher-level thinking and reading skills so essential in a culture of diverse and contradictory opinions.

In addition to providing a tool for critical thinking, Opposing Viewpoints books challenge readers to question their own strongly held opinions and assumptions. Most people form their opinions on the basis of upbringing, peer pressure, and personal, cultural, or professional bias. By reading carefully balanced opposing views, readers must directly confront new ideas as well as the opinions of those with whom they disagree. This is not to simplistically argue that everyone who reads opposing views will—or should—change his or her opinion. Instead, the series enhances readers' understanding of their own views by encouraging confrontation with opposing ideas. Careful examination of others' views can lead to the readers' understanding of the logical inconsistencies in their own opinions, perspective on why they hold an opinion, and the consideration of the possibility that their opinion requires further evaluation.

Evaluating Other Opinions

To ensure that this type of examination occurs, Opposing Viewpoints books present all types of opinions. Prominent spokespeople on different sides of each issue as well as well-known professionals from many disciplines challenge the reader. An additional goal of the series is to provide a forum for other, less known, or even unpopular viewpoints. The opinion of an ordinary person who has had to make the decision to cut off life support from a terminally ill relative, for example, may be just as valuable and provide just as much insight as a medical ethicist's professional opinion. The editors have two additional purposes in including these less known views. One, the editors encourage readers to respect others' opinions—even when not enhanced by professional credibility. It is only by reading or listening to and objectively evaluating others' ideas that one can determine whether they are worthy of consideration. Two, the inclusion of such viewpoints encourages the important critical thinking skill of objectively evaluating an author's credentials and bias. This evaluation will illuminate an author's reasons for taking a particular stance on an issue and will aid in readers' evaluation of the author's ideas.

It is our hope that these books will give readers a deeper understanding of the issues debated and an appreciation of the complexity of even seemingly simple issues when good and honest people disagree. This awareness is particularly important in a democratic society such as ours in which people enter into public debate to determine the common good. Those with whom one disagrees should not be regarded as enemies but rather as people whose views deserve careful examination and may shed light on one's own.

Thomas Jefferson once said that "difference of opinion leads to inquiry, and inquiry to truth." Jefferson, a broadly educated man, argued that "if a nation expects to be ignorant and free . . . it expects what never was and never will be." As individuals and as a nation, it is imperative that we consider the opinions of others and examine them with skill and discernment. The Opposing Viewpoints Series is intended to help readers achieve this goal.

David L. Bender and Bruno Leone,
Founders

Introduction

> *"[There is] a traditional Chinese saying that there are three solutions to women's problems: 'one—to cry; two—to scream; and three—to hang herself.'"*
>
> Bulletin of the World
> Health Organization, *December 2009*

In China, suicide and gender are connected in disturbing ways. Worldwide, suicide rates tend to be higher in urban areas and among males. In China, by contrast, rural women are disproportionately likely to commit suicide. In fact, according to a December 2009 article on the website of the World Health Organization (WHO), suicide is the leading cause of death for young women in rural China. WHO reports that a woman attempts suicide every four minutes in China.

Why are women, and especially rural women, so prone to suicide in China? Commentators have suggested a number of possible explanations. Namrata Hasija, in a September 26, 2011, post at the Institute of Peace and Conflict Studies website, argues that the opening up of the Chinese economy, and the resultant immigration of many men to cities, has left women stranded and isolated in rural areas. In a May 15, 2007, article in the *Washington Post*, Maureen Fan links high suicide rates in China to rural poverty and traditional views of marriage and male authority. Such views can encourage, and make it difficult for women to escape from, domestic abuse, she notes. Fan points also to a 2002 study showing that 38 percent of women who attempted suicide in China reported being beaten by their husbands.

Heidi Miller, in a March 29, 2012, article at LifeNews.com, also links the high suicide rate to women's low status. Miller argues in particular that China's one-child policy, which restricts the number of children each family can have, leads to depression and a contempt for women. "Imagine a woman who desperately wants her daughter, but has that daughter forcibly stripped from her womb," Miller says. "This does not sound like preservation of the value and dignity of a female life. This sounds like hopelessness and despair."

In addition to the low status and poverty of women, other aspects of rural life in China make suicide dangerously easy. Toxic pesticides banned in many parts of the world are frequently encountered on farms in China. Often the pesticides are kept in jars in outhouses, according to a June 16, 2010, article by Megan Shank at the *Daily Beast*. Shank reports that 60 percent of Chinese suicides involved pesticides. She notes that worldwide, female suicide rates are higher than for males, but that males are more often successful in their attempts. Pesticides, however, are a very effective method of suicide. Chinese women who try to kill themselves with these substances often succeed.

Problems with health care in rural China may also contribute to female suicides. Shank points out that many rural physicians are not equipped to deal with the results of pesticide poisoning. Namrata Hasija at the Institute of Peace and Conflict Studies also notes that doctors in rural China often minimize mental health issues or depression, making it difficult to identify suicide risks early on. Hasija also says that there is a strong stigma against discussing family or domestic matters with outsiders. This prevents women from seeking help when they need it.

There is some evidence, however, that suicides among Chinese women may be decreasing. In 2008, the Chinese Ministry of Agriculture put new regulations on pesticides. Women are also migrating to the city, where they may have more opportunities, as well as less access to pesticides. China's economic boom, which has improved living standards for all, may also be a factor.

Increased economic opportunity can sometimes be a cause of depression in itself, however. An October 16, 2003, article in the *Guardian*, a Manchester, England, newspaper, for example, reports on a woman named Mei-Hua, who attempted suicide after moving away from the country and her abusive husband. When asked why she tried to kill herself, she replied:

> Why? I didn't know that there was such a different life here compared with my village. Then I thought about it all the time. Why have I not had the chance to learn to read and write in my life? Why do I have no right to choose whom I love—because I am a second-class citizen? Why did I have to give up my baby girl, while the daughters of city people dress beautifully and walk around arm-in-arm with young boys? How can I face them with the daily pain of my missing daughter?
>
> Why? What is wrong with my life? Why is my fate so poor? Why? Why?!

The growing inequality caused by economic reform, then, can be a source of despair in itself. Perhaps that is part of the reason that, as Hasija reports, high suicide rates among women in China remain a serious problem.

The viewpoints in this book will present other examples of gendercide under the following chapter headings: What Are Common Practices of Gendercide in Developing Countries?, What Are Common Practices of Gendercide in Developed Countries?, What Is the Relationship Between Gender-Related Violence and Genocide?, and Who Is the Target of Gendercide? In each chapter, the authors debate how different policies, cultures, and attitudes contribute to gendercide, and what changes can be made to reduce this horror.

What Are Common Practices of Gendercide in Developing Countries?

Chapter Preface

Sons in India are seen as valuable both because they work and provide for their parents in old age and because girls customarily are required to pay expensive dowries when they marry. The combination of these factors can make the birth of a baby girl a crippling economic burden for a poor family. To avoid this, families have sometimes resorted to infanticide, killing their newborn daughters. According to Adam Jones's article on infanticide on the website Gendercide Watch, baby girls are sometimes fed poisonous fertilizer or unhulled rice which punctures their windpipe. They may also be suffocated with a damp towel, or allowed to starve. Many, according to Ranjani Iyer Mohanty in a May 25, 2012, article in the *Atlantic Monthly*, are simply abandoned, to be discovered "in alleyways, outside temples and churches, in shopping malls and public bathrooms, and inside garbage cans."

Activists and authorities have worked to reduce female infanticide through education, through outlawing dowries, and through raising the status of women. Mohanty discusses another effort—baby hatches. These are safe places, like cribs or rooms, where parents can leave children with no questions asked and no threat of prosecution. The babies are then raised by the government, or placed with adoptive families. Baby hatches have been used in both Europe and America, and there is hope that introducing them in India could encourage some families to turn their babies over to the state rather than killing them.

Unfortunately, the problem of infanticide is not restricted to newborns. Indian girls continue to be in danger for many years. While 12 million girls are born in India, a million die before they are a year old. A UN study found that India was the deadliest place for girl children in the world; Indian girls between one and five years old were 75 percent more likely to die than boys of the same age.

The viewpoints in this chapter will examine sex-selective abortion in China and India—a form of gendercide encouraged by many of the same factors that contribute to infanticide and the murder of young girls.

| *"For millions of couples [in the developing world], the answer is: abort the daughter, try for a son."*

Sex-Selective Abortion Is Leading to Unprecedented Gendercide in the Developing World

The Economist

The Economist *is a weekly British news publication covering business and politics and that traditionally does not use author bylines. In the following viewpoint, the author reports on the preference for sons in developing countries like China and India. The preference leads many families to use ultrasounds to determine the sex of children before birth, and then to abort female fetuses. This has a serious destabilizing effect on society since large surpluses of men can result in higher crime rates and violence. To address these problems,* The Economist *recommends looking to South Korea, where the rising status of women has reduced the prejudice against daughters.* The Economist *also says that China should abandon its one-child-per-family policy, which only exacerbates the gendercide of girls.*

As you read, consider the following questions:

1. For what reasons does *The Economist* argue that large numbers of single young men are especially destabilizing for Asian societies?

2. According to the author, why does increasing wealth and prosperity not necessarily reduce the gendercide against girls?

3. What does the author suggest that countries do to raise the value of girls?

Imagine you are one half of a young couple expecting your first child in a fast-growing, poor country. You are part of the new middle class; your income is rising; you want a small family. But traditional *mores* hold sway around you, most important in the preference for sons over daughters. Perhaps hard physical labour is still needed for the family to make its living. Perhaps only sons may inherit land. Perhaps a daughter is deemed to join another family on marriage and you want someone to care for you when you are old. Perhaps she needs a dowry.

Now imagine that you have had an ultrasound scan; it costs $12, but you can afford that. The scan says the unborn child is a girl. You yourself would prefer a boy; the rest of your family clamours for one. You would never dream of killing a baby daughter, as they do out in the villages. But an abortion seems different. What do you do?

Abort the Daughter, Try for a Son

For millions of couples, the answer is: abort the daughter, try for a son. In China and northern India more than 120 boys are being born for every 100 girls. Nature dictates that slightly more males are born than females to offset boys' greater susceptibility to infant disease. But nothing on this scale.

For those who oppose abortion, this is mass murder. For those such as this newspaper, who think abortion should be "safe, legal and rare" (to use [former US president] Bill Clinton's phrase), a lot depends on the circumstances, but the cumulative consequence for societies of such individual actions is catastrophic. China alone stands to have as many unmarried young men—"bare branches", as they are known—as the entire population of young men in America. In any country rootless young males spell trouble; in Asian societies, where marriage and children are the recognised routes into society, single men are almost like outlaws. Crime rates, bride trafficking, sexual violence, even female suicide rates are all rising and will rise further as the lopsided generations reach their maturity.

It is no exaggeration to call this gendercide. Women are missing in their millions—aborted, killed, neglected to death. In 1990 an Indian economist, Amartya Sen, put the number at 100m[million]; the toll is higher now. The crumb of comfort is that countries can mitigate the hurt, and that one, South Korea, has shown the worst can be avoided. Others need to learn from it if they are to stop the carnage.

The Dearth and Death of Sisters

Most people know China and northern India have unnaturally large numbers of boys. But few appreciate how bad the problem is, or that it is rising. In China the imbalance between the sexes was 108 boys to 100 girls for the generation born in the late 1980s; for the generation of the early 2000s, it was 124 to 100. In some Chinese provinces the ratio is an unprecedented 130 to 100. The destruction is worst in China but has spread far beyond. Other East Asian countries, including Taiwan and Singapore, former communist states in the western Balkans and the Caucasus, and even sections of America's population (Chinese- and Japanese-Americans, for example): all these have distorted sex ratios. Gendercide exists on almost every continent. It affects rich and poor; educated and illiterate; Hindu, Muslim, Confucian and Christian alike.

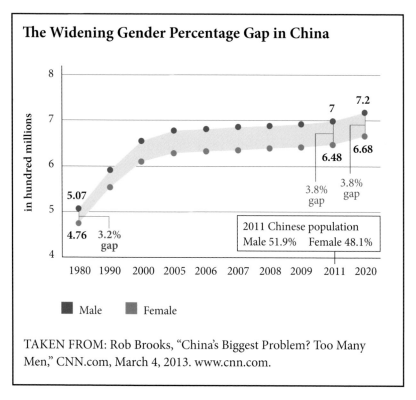

The Widening Gender Percentage Gap in China

TAKEN FROM: Rob Brooks, "China's Biggest Problem? Too Many Men," CNN.com, March 4, 2013. www.cnn.com.

Wealth does not stop it. Taiwan and Singapore have open, rich economies. Within China and India the areas with the worst sex ratios are the richest, best-educated ones. And China's one-child policy can only be part of the problem, given that so many other countries are affected.

In fact the destruction of baby girls is a product of three forces: the ancient preference for sons; a modern desire for smaller families; and ultrasound scanning and other technologies that identify the sex of a fetus. In societies where four or six children were common, a boy would almost certainly come along eventually; son preference did not need to exist at the expense of daughters. But now couples want two children—or, as in China, are allowed only one—they will sacrifice unborn daughters to their pursuit of a son. That is why sex ratios are most distorted in the modern, open parts of China and India. It is also why ratios are more skewed after the first child: parents may accept a daughter first time round but will do anything to ensure their next—and probably last—child is a boy. The boy-girl ratio is above 200 for a third child in some places.

A Malign Combination

Baby girls are thus victims of a malign combination of ancient prejudice and modern preferences for small families. Only one country has managed to change this pattern. In the 1990s South Korea had a sex ratio almost as skewed as China's. Now, it is heading towards normality. It has achieved this not deliberately, but because the culture changed. Female education, anti-discrimination suits and equal-rights rulings made son preference seem old-fashioned and unnecessary. The forces of modernity first exacerbated prejudice—then overwhelmed it.

But this happened when South Korea was rich. If China or India—with incomes one-quarter and one-tenth Korea's levels—wait until they are as wealthy, many generations will pass. To speed up change, they need to take actions that are in their own interests anyway. Most obviously China should scrap the one-child policy. The country's leaders will resist this because they fear population growth; they also dismiss Western concerns about human rights. But the one-child limit is no longer needed to reduce fertility (if it ever was: other East Asian countries reduced the pressure on the population as much as China). And it massively distorts the country's sex ratio, with devastating results. President Hu Jintao says that creating "a harmonious society" is his guiding principle; it cannot be achieved while a policy so profoundly perverts family life.

And all countries need to raise the value of girls. They should encourage female education; abolish laws and customs that prevent daughters [from] inheriting property; make examples of hospitals and clinics with impossible sex ratios; get women engaged in public life—using everything from television newsreaders to women traffic police. [Communist China's first leader] Mao Zedong said "women hold up half the sky." The world needs to do more to prevent a gendercide that will have the sky crashing down.

"As everyone familiar with India's history knows, female infanticide has a
long tradition ... [and] that Asia's sex
ratio is at an unprecedented high ... is
clearly wrong."

Sex Selection in the Developing World Today Is Neither Unprecedented nor Gendercide

Edgar Dahl

Edgar Dahl is spokesman for the German Society for Reproductive Medicine and the editor of Giving Death a Helping Hand: Physician-Assisted Suicide and Public Policy. *In the following viewpoint he rebuts an argument by* The Economist *that lopsided gender ratios in the developing world have not been caused by ultrasound technology and abortion. Rather, he contends, there is a long history of infanticide of baby girls in China and India, and a long history of gender imbalances. The problem, he argues, is not technology, but religious and economic factors that*

Edgar Dahl, "Gendercide? A Commentary on *The Economist*'s Report About Worldwide War on Baby Girls," *Journal of Evolution and Technology*, vol. 21, no. 2, October 2010, pp. 20–22. Copyright © 2010 by Journal of Evolution and Technology. All rights reserved. Reproduced by permission.

bestow privilege on sons. He suggests using technological advantages in sperm sorting to ensure that women give birth to boys as a way to avoid abortion and infanticide.

As you read, consider the following questions:

1. What evidence does Dahl provide to show that Asia's male-to-female sex ratio is not at an unprecedented high?

2. Why does Dahl believe that wealthy people in India are more likely to invest in sons than daughters?

3. According to Dahl, what are Chinese and Indian parents' attitudes toward having a daughter as their first child?

There is an old Indian proverb according to which "eighteen goddess-like daughters are not equal to one son with a hump." In its recent article "Gendercide: The Worldwide War on Baby Girls," *The Economist* reported about the gruesome fate of daughters in countries like China, Korea and India. As is well-known, girls are still ruthlessly discriminated against in large parts of the Asian continent and the Arab world. The most outrageous crime against daughters is infanticide—the killing of newborn babies for no other reason than being of the "wrong" sex.

A Long Tradition of Infanticide

Although I welcome *The Economist*'s effort to keep us aware of the discrimination against baby girls, its article is highly misleading. First, it seems to imply that the advent of science and technology has made things worse in Asia. However, as everyone familiar with India's history knows, female infanticide has a long tradition. For example, in the nineteenth century the Jhareja Rajputs killed virtually all their girls at birth. They were even known as the "kuri mar," the "daughter killers." One of the most important reasons for preferring sons over daughters is religion. According to Hinduism, a man who has failed to sire a son cannot achieve salvation. Only a male descendant can light the funeral pyre and ensure the redemption of the departed soul. Thus, the fault does not lie with science but with religion.

Second, the article suggests that Asia's sex ratio is at an unprecedented high. This is clearly wrong. In the eighteenth and nineteenth centuries, China's sex ratios were as high as 154:100. As famous biologist Sarah Blaffer Hrdy writes in her brilliant book *Mother Nature*: "In large cities like Beijing, wagons made scheduled rounds in the early morning to collect corpses of unwanted daughters that had been soundlessly drowned in a bucket of milk while the mother looked away."

Third, it underestimates the economic logic behind the son preference. In India, it is clearly the tradition of dowry that makes daughters unwanted. The dowry payments are considerable. They extend from US$3,000 to US$125,000. To marry off one or more daughters is therefore a huge financial burden. Since girls are a liability and boys are an asset, it should not come as a surprise that Indian couples prefer sons over daughters. In other countries, it is a son's labor value that makes parents long for a boy. Or, as an old Tibetan proverb has it "Daughters are no better than crows. Their parents feed them and when they get their wings, they fly away."

Exaggerated Effects

Fourth, it exaggerates the social implications of sex ratio distortions. It is far from obvious that "bare branches" [the Chinese term for unmarried men] will turn out to be a political hazard. An overabundance of men is anything but new. In his excellent book *Violent Land: Single Men and Social Disorder from the Frontier to the Inner City*, historian David T. Courtwright has shown that societies in which men outnumber women do not necessarily wreak havoc. For example, in the

Infanticide in Chinese History

The prevalence of female infanticide in China can be traced to the low regard for girls that dated from Chinese antiquity. The *Book of Odes (Shijing)* is one of the oldest Chinese classics, dating from ca. 1000 BC to ca. 600 BC. . . . Ode 189 . . . expresses this differing regard for boys and girls in the following verses.

> So he bears a son,
> And puts him to sleep upon a
> bed,
> Clothes him in robes,
> Gives him a jade scepter to play
> with,
> The child's howling is very lusty;
> In red greaves shall he flare,
> Be lord and king of house and
> home.
> Then he bears a daughter,
> And puts her upon the ground,
> Clothes her in swaddling-clothes,
> Gives her a loom-whorl to play
> with.
> For her no decorations, no em-
> blames;
> Her only care, the wine and food
> And how to give no trouble to
> father and mother

The different treatment of boys and girls reflected different expectations of what each one would cost and contribute to the family, and this attitude would later contribute to female infanticide.

D.E. Mungello, Drowning Girls in China:
Female Infanticide in China Since 1650, *2008.*

Wild West of America unmarried men "were put to doing hard, dangerous work, such as building railroads and canals."

Fifth, that sexual disparities rise with income is anything but a "puzzle." This is exactly what evolutionary theory predicts. As biologist Robert Trivers and mathematician Dan Willard pointed out some 30 years ago, rich parents are more likely to invest in sons and poor families are more likely to invest in daughters. The reason is simple enough. Given that all living beings are designed by natural selection, we are programmed to spread our genes. If it is all about successful reproduction, rich parents are clearly better off investing in boys than in girls. No matter how much money a girl has, she will only give birth to a handful of children, while a wealthy boy can sire literally hundreds of children. Apart from biology, even economy can account for the fact that wealthy Indians are more inclined to have boys than girls. The richer they are the more expensive it gets to marry off a daughter.

Sixth, . . . that Asia's high sex ratios are the result of a "fateful collision between overweening son preference, the use of rapidly spreading prenatal sex-determination technology and declining fertility." However, he is surely wrong in claiming that discrimination against girls is a "global trend." Just look at Americans. If there is a preference at all, it is a growing preference for girls. Similarly, more than 70 per cent of Japanese women prefer daughters over sons.

Technology Is the Solution

Seventh, and finally, technology might not be the problem but the solution to high sex ratios and sex discrimination. . . . The sex ratios of firstborn children in China are "within the bounds of normality." The same applies to India. It is only the sex ratio for the second, third or fourth child that is severely distorted. This means that first-born daughters are not discriminated against. Or, as Monica Das Gupta put it: they are "treated the same as their brothers." Consequently, . . . "The rule seems to be that parents will joyfully embrace a daughter as their first child. But they will go to extraordinary lengths to ensure that subsequent children are sons." Given that Indian and Chinese parents have strong religious and economic incentives for having boys, their preferences are entirely rational.

So how about helping Indian and Chinese parents to ensure the birth of a son? Instead of criminalizing sex selection we could regulate sex selection. For instance, we could restrict the use of sex selection technology to couples already having at least one daughter. This way the parents of daughters do not have to worry. Using MicroSort, a safe and reliable technology that allows to separate X-bearing from Y-bearing sperm, they could trust they will get the son they need. Isn't better to eliminate X-bearing sperm than to kill daughters?

Who is supposed to pay for this kind of high-tech sex selection? I am sure if the Indian government were to invest their money on technology rather than on enforcing their unenforceable *Prohibition of Sex Selection Act*, there would be enough for everyone.

| "When policies reduce fertility to one or two children only, the incentive for sex selective abortion, neglect, or, in worst cases, infanticide is enhanced."

China's One-Child Policy Has Contributed to the Abortion of Girls

Anu Liisanantti and Karin Beese

Anu Liisanantti is a program officer for the Overseas Development Institute in Great Britain; Karin Beese is a project manager at the Ecologic Institute in Germany. *In the following viewpoint, they argue that women have a traditionally low status in China and that this has led to infanticide and abortion of girls. China's one-child policy, which limits the number of children couples can have, has made matters even worse. The authors assert that China has made some progress in reducing its gender imbalance through regulations and educational campaigns to raise the status of women.*

As you read, consider the following questions:

1. According to the authors, how does Confucian philosophy support the low status of women?

Anu Liisanantti and Karin Beese, "Gendercide: The Missing Women," European Parliament Directorate-General for External Policies, March 2012.

2. What are some exceptions to the one-child policy in China, according to the authors?

3. What specific actions did China take in 1995 and 2000 to promote gender equality, according to Liisanantti and Beese?

Researchers have long been concerned with the unusually high ratio of males to females in the Chinese population. The high gender disparity particularly among Chinese newborns has caught the attention of demographic experts nationally and internationally since the mid-1990s, following [economist] Amartya Sen's findings in the early 1990s. Although rapid industrialisation and declining fertility have reshaped China in the past four decades, sex preferences seem to have survived the transition.

[Researchers S.] Tiefenbrun and [T.] Edwards in 2008, amongst others, have studied the interconnection of historic, legal and cultural features that result in the perpetuation of discrimination against women in Chinese society. According to their analysis, China is facing a demographic crisis, as women are "bought and sold, murdered and made to disappear in order to comply with a governmental policy that coincides with the cultural phenomenon of male-child preference".

Women's Status in Chinese Society

Daughters are like water that splashes out of the family and cannot be gotten back after marriage. (Traditional Chinese proverb)

Women's inferiority is deeply ingrained in the Chinese culture, supported by the Confucian view of a virtuous woman upholding 'three subordinations': be subordinate to her father before marriage, to her husband after marriage, and to her son after her husband died. In traditional Chinese rural society, only sons can inherit family properties and host their parents' funeral ceremonies, as well as carry on family names (a common practice in many countries worldwide), and consequently having a son is extremely important to the family. The strict patrilineal family system (child belongs to the father's lineage) vests responsibilities upon male offspring for economic-socio cultural and religious functions.

In Chinese culture, girls typically marry into the husband's family, leave home, and are expected to take care of their husband's parents. Since only boys can continue the patrilineal family line, girl babies are seen as financial burdens, unable to look after their elderly parents who don't get sufficient economic support from the inadequate social services system. Women have to depend on men, which results in women's low status. [Canadian anthropologist Laurel] Bossen has pointed out that Chinese women have often been portrayed as a unified group sharing the same experience of devaluation and subordination to males. To a great extent, state policies also affect equity of sexes. When male-dominated family power is replaced by a country's male-dominated social systems, laws, ideologies and resource allocation, control over women becomes part of the public patriarchy. This combination of both private and public patriarchy constitutes an entirely dominant system, which keeps women in a firmly subordinate position.

While women's status has greatly improved in contemporary China, traditional culture and customs delay this process, and the problem cannot be solved merely through economic development, as also seen in the case of India.

China's One-Child Policy

Historically, Chinese parents have favoured large families and have often directed family resources to sons at the expense of daughters. However, the status of women was recognised during the leadership of Mao Zedong (also Mao Tse Tung), the founder of the People's Republic of China, who stayed in power from 1949 until his death in 1976. Mao's proclamation "Women hold up half of the sky" reflects his view that there could be no emancipation of humanity without the participation and emancipation of women. Furthermore, in 1955, Mao insisted that "In order to build a great socialist society it is of the utmost importance to arouse the broad masses of women to join in productive activity. Men and women must receive equal pay for equal work in production. Genuine equality between the sexes can only be realized in the process of the socialist transformation of society as a whole."

As the population grew rapidly, Chinese policymakers felt compelled to limit fertility, and the post-Mao Communist Party began enacting a series of fertility control policies, culminating in the one-child policy (OCP) in 1979. It is argued that the family planning became a revolutionary motto that took hold of the people by subtle forms of brainwashing, evidenced by advertisements, billboards, books, cartoons, movies, news, paintings etc. The sacrifice of having only one child became routinely glorified as obedience to duty and expression of love of one's country.

Missing Women

OCP, referred in China as "family planning law", applies currently to approximately 60% of China's population, officially restricting married, urban couples to having only one child, while allowing exemptions for several cases, including rural couples, ethnic minorities, and parents without any siblings themselves. The policy is enforced at the provincial level through fines that are imposed based on the income of the family and other factors. The result of varying fertility policies is an effective national fertility policy of 1.47 children per couple.

Analyses of trends in the sex ratio at birth in China have highlighted the importance of the OCP as a key moment in the rise of sex ratios at birth, and many studies have explored the contribution of OCP in distorting sex ratios. When OCP meets the traditional preference for sons, the outcome can often be either sex selective abortion or abandonment. Families that need a son may keep their first daughter and try again (most rural families are allowed to have a second child if their first child is a girl—a telling exception to the policy). However if they bear another girl, abandonment may be their only option.

Focusing on Chinese families with more than one child, [a number of researchers have] demonstrate[d] that sex ratios at birth (SRB) are not only increasing consistently with birth order, but actually vary by the sex composition of the existing children in the household. In other words, and similarly to India, although sex ratios are close to normal for first births, the sex ratio for second, third and fourth births is strikingly different, especially depending on the sex of the first-born. . . . SRB tends to increase with birth order.

Recent estimates suggest that as many as 40 million women are "missing" in China, and it is argued that OCP is responsible for about half of these cases, even before the ultrasound technologies for prenatal sex determination were available. [Researchers E.] Bulte et al. in 2010 looked in detail into the interaction between OCP and distorted sex ratios. Their study shows that when policies reduce fertility to one or two children only, the incentive for sex selective abortion, neglect, or, in worst cases, infanticide is enhanced when the (prospective) offspring's sex is of the "wrong type", in this case, female. Non-registration for the first or second infant is also common. In rural districts of China, the family planning rules are strictly enforced. Many women are afraid of the social stigma and large fines and penalties imposed on them for violating the one- or two-child limit. While families may be willing to pay the fine if a son is born, most would not consider paying fines for a daughter.

Prenatal Discrimination

A consensus has emerged that the sex ratio distribution in China is due to prenatal discrimination against female conceptions. The consensus is based on evidence from fertility surveys, field work and census data. The discrimination leads directly to the phenomenon of "missing girls". From the census in 1990, [researchers] estimated the number of missing girls to be 34.6 million, and the percentage of missing girls to be 6.3 percent. According to the 2000 census, the estimated number of China's missing girls was 40.9 million, reaching 6.7 percent.

Recent evidence from China—data collected by the inter-census survey in 2005—[shows that], while sex ratios were high across all age groups and residence, they were highest in the 1–4 age group. They estimated that in 2005 there were 32 million more males than females under the age of 20 in China, and that 1.1 million excess male births occurred that year. While there is a lack of reliable national data, findings at the sub-national level reveal high disparities in sex ratios at birth. Analysis of recent data shows that while SRB is more skewed in rural areas, the ratios in large cities (Beijing, Tianjin and Shanghai) had increased between 2000 and 2005.

[Researchers S.] Anderson and [D.] Ray, who have studied the distribution of "missing women" by age and disease in both China and India, discovered that the two countries have distinct age profiles of missing women. According to their study, a large percentage of missing women in China are indeed located before birth and in infancy, estimating that around 37–45% of China's missing women are due to prenatal factors alone. This finding is supported by researchers at Peking and Tsinghua University, who collected new data that tracks the differential diffusion of diagnostic ultrasound and used data on recorded births. They conclude that the skewed sex ratios at birth are significantly influenced by prenatal sex selection and that the effect of ultrasound on child gender is predominantly a result of prenatal sex selection in areas under tougher enforcement of birth control when the one child policy was effective. It needs to be noted, however, that the relevant data relating to sex selective abortions are not easy to find especially in rural areas because the majority of these cases take place in secret.

Second-Order Births and Trafficking

A [2011] paper by [researcher Z.] Wenhua finds strong association between son preference and second birth fertility in China, echoing the studies conducted in India, regardless of the OCP. "The rather skewed sex ratio of second birth implies that son preference accounts very much for the motive to progress to second birth for Chinese women." His analysis reveals a very clear motive that lacking a son triggers women in China to renew their child-bearing despite the fines associated with breaching the one-child regulations. This seems to indicate that households are willing to pay the fines for a male offspring.

Some studies suggest that sex selection, fuelled by male preference, has already led to increased trafficking of girls and women. Trafficking has many forms: the purchasing of women for brides, the purchase of a male son, or the sale of unwanted female children. Human trafficking in China is a lucrative international business that is expanding due to several factors: the aggressive implementation of the OCP, a faulty legal system, and the uncritical adherence to long-standing cultural traditions that devalue women. . . .

Government and Social Responses

To protect women's rights and promote gender equality, the Chinese government has introduced a series of laws and regulations on equal rights regarding economic and political participation, education, property inheritance, marriage and old-age support. China outlawed sex-selective abortions in 1995

Sex Ratios at Birth by Birth Order in China, 2005

Parity (order of birth)	Sex ratio at birth (boys per 100 girls)
1st born	108.4
2nd	143.2
3rd	156.4
4th	141.8

Data adapted from China's population census and population sample survey in 2005.

TAKEN FROM: Anu Liisanantti and Karin Beese, "Gendercide: The Missing Women," European Parliament Directorate-General for External Policies, March 2012, p. 21. www.ecologic.eu/4760.

and in 2000 undertook a pilot campaign to raise awareness of the value of girls called "Care for Girls", which aimed to "improve the environment for girls' survival and development." The programme was initiated with support from the Information, Education and Communication Department of the former State Family Planning Commission (the present National Population and Family Planning Commission) and the Population and Economic Research Institute of Xi'an Jiaotong University.

This programme includes: financial help for 1- and 2-daughter families; sponsoring of girls' educational fees and increased pensions to families with daughters. Since the introduction of the program in Chaohu (a city in Anhui province), the local SRB went from 125 in 1999 to 114 in 2002. In response to this apparent success, the government expanded the program to 24 counties with high SRB rates in 2003–2004, and saw the average SRB in those counties drop from 133.8 in 2000 to 119.6 in 2005. Stipulation and initiation of a national "Care for Girls" campaign occurred in January 2006–July 2006, with the goal of bringing the national SRB average to normal levels within 15 years. In January 2008, the government expanded on this effort by launching the "Care for Girls Youth Volunteer Action", beginning with more than 1000 students (mostly at the university level) directed at engaging in promotional activities and data collection (under the Chinese Communist Youth League).

So far, according to the UN inter-agency statement on gender-biased sex selection, these measures have had only limited results. In August 2011, a nation-wide, 18-month campaign was launched, aiming at raising awareness on gender equality, severely punishing those involved in sex selective abortions and improving monitoring of medical institutions and practitioners. During the campaign from August 2011 to March 2012, efforts will be made to raise awareness of gender equality, to severely punish those involved in cases of non-medical sex determinations and sex-selective abortions, and to strengthen monitoring. "Doctors who violate the ban will be stripped of licenses or penalized, and involved medical institutions will also be given harsh punishments", said Liu Qian, vice minister of the Ministry of Health

Many national intervention projects have not only been supported by local and central governments in China, but also by a broad spectrum of national and international research and civil-society organisations. Supported by international organisations . . . some research institutes have collaborated with the government to study gender-based issues. The Asia Foundation currently assists civil-society organisations and the government to adapt to a new era of open politics and citizen participation, and to support further democratisation and socio-economic reform. NGOs [nongovernmental organizations], such as the All-China Women's Federation (ACWF) and the Population and Family Planning Association (PFPAC), also play a role in relevant national policymaking. This is particularly so in the corresponding monitoring that needs to take place, as well as in representing and protecting women's rights, and promoting international exchanges. The category of civilian organisations also includes women's organisations in academic, service and other domains; these usually focus on one specific problem concerning gender equity and women's development, and have been well developed since the 1990s. All in all, NGOs and civilian organisations could play increasingly important roles in improving women's development, and in ensuring environments conducive to girls' survival.

| *"India's already skewed infant sex ratio is getting worse."*

Abortion of Girls Is a Problem in India

Gursharan Singh Kainth

Gursharan Singh Kainth is the director of the Guru Arjan Dev Institute of Development Studies. In the following viewpoint, he argues that sex-selective abortion in India is causing the loss of a generation of girls. He contends that sex ratios in India actually seem to be worsening and that increased wealth and a desire for smaller families is exacerbating the situation. He maintains that the imbalance of girls will make Indian society unstable and threatens the development both of India and of the region.

As you read, consider the following questions:

1. In which areas of India does Kainth say that sex selection did not used to be a problem but is now becoming more common?

2. What evidence does the author provide that India's skewed sex ratio may be making things worse for women?

3. According to Kainth, what are some signs of hope that the aborting of girls may be slowing or turning around in India?

The result of the 2011 census of India is almost all heartening. Literacy is up; life expectancy is up; family size is stabilizing. But there is one grim exception—India's already skewed infant sex ratio is getting worse. India counted only 914 girls aged six and under for every 1,000 boys or 75.8m [million] girls and 82.9m boys. This sex ratio is the worst in the recorded history of the modern Indian.

India's Sex Ratio Is Worsening

According to 1991 census, the 0–6 sex ratio was 934 girls to 1,000 boys, which decline to 927 as per 2001 census. Nature provides that slightly more boys are born than girls: the normal sex ratio for children aged 0–6 is about 952 girls per 1,000 boys. Fast growth, urbanization and surging literacy seem not to have affected the trend. A cultural preference for sons and the increasing availability of prenatal screening to determine a baby's sex have helped contribute to a worsening in the ratio, which has been deteriorating rapidly even as the ratio for the population as a whole has improved. A decline was recorded in 28 of the country's 35 states and Union Territories, among which there is wide variation; from 830 in the northern state of Haryana to 973 in Meghalaya in the east. . . . The sex-ratio is most distorted in the states of the northern Gangetic Plain, such as Punjab.

Haryana, West Bengal, remains the direst of all, with only 830 girls per 1,000 boys. More worrying, places that used not to discriminate in favour of sons, such as the poorer central and north-eastern states, have begun to do so. Economic success seems to spread son preference to places that were once more neutral about the sex composition of their children. The new census showed a worsening sex ratio in all but eight of

India's 35 states and territories (though those eight include some of the most extreme examples, for instance, Punjab). Female literacy, improving general health care, improving female employment rates are slowly redefining motherhood from childbearing to child rearing—an indication that the country has reached a point of inflection. New Delhi [India's capital] launched a round of policy initiatives designed to turn the situation around.

Cradle baby schemes, where girl babies can be left anonymously at government buildings, were instituted in some states. In the north and northwest, where the worst sex ratios were found, state governments paid cash to families that chose to keep their girls and offered additional money if the girls were immunized, sent to school and not married off before 18 years of age. Government officials have condemned the culling of daughters from the population, as have religious leaders. Some Sikh and Hindu priests have even administered oaths to their followers not to engage in this practice.

Whatever success these efforts may have had, they are apparently not enough. Indeed, as the average family size drops in India, the preference for sons only intensifies. It is sons who inherit land, pass on the family name, financially provide for parents in old age and perform rituals for deceased parents.

Daughters, on the other hand, will cost the family dearly at the time of their marriage, with a dowry at times costing as much as a family makes in a year. For all of these reasons, as families choose to have fewer children, they try to ensure the presence of a sufficient number of sons—and as few daughters as possible.

Girls Are Equated with Birth Defects

As a result, it becomes tantamount to having a serious birth defect in the minds of Indian parents, with genuine sentiment for their daughters giving way to a stifling economic calculus.

But as daughters become rarer, they will become more valued. But dowry costs in India are rising, not falling, and the ratio of girls to boys continues to fall dramatically. In the area dubbed the "Bermuda Triangle for girls" in India, some districts register only 774 little girls for every 1,000 boys, a ratio of almost 130 boys to every 100 girls. Though the sex ratio has been worsening for decades, it is doing so more slowly. The figure in 2001 was 1.9 per cent worse than it had been in 1991. The figure in 2011 was 1.5 per cent worse than in 2001—an improvement of sorts.

The impact on Indian society is grim. One might have thought that scarcity would lead to girls being valued more highly, but this is not happening. One measure is the practice of giving dowries. Almost no one, rich or poor, urban or rural, dreams of dispensing with these. Rather, as Indians grow wealthier, dowries are getting more lavish and are spreading to places where they were once rare, such as in Tamil Nadu and Kerala, in the south. The majority of women shake their heads when asked to imagine life without dowries. The simple answer was: Nobody would find a husband.

If we compare the number of girls actually born to the number that would have been born had a normal sex ratio prevailed, then 600,000 Indian girls go missing every year. This is less distorted than the sex ratio in China. However, China's ratio has stabilized; India's is widening, and has been for decades. Sex selection is now invading parts of the country that used not to practice it.

India's sex ratio shows that gendercide is a feature not just of dictatorship and poverty. Unlike China, India is a democracy: there is no one-child policy to blame. Although parts of the country are poor, poverty alone does not explain India's preference for sons. The states with the worst sex ratios—Punjab, Haryana, Gujarat—are among the richest, which suggests distorted sex selection will not be corrected just by wealth or government policy. But it can be corrected.

Something Has to Give

Parents choose to abort female fetuses not because they do not want or love their daughters, but because they feel they must have sons (usually for social reasons): they also want smaller families—and something has to give. Ultrasound technology ensures that this something is a generation of unborn daughters, because it lets them know the sex of a fetus. Sex selection therefore tends to increase with education and income: wealthier, better educated people are more likely to want fewer children and can more easily afford the scans—disastrous for the nation.

The "missing girls" are usually aborted, shortly after the parents learn of their sex. No doubt, the requests for a scan to check the sex of a fetus are turned down at a majority of Ultrasound centers and hospitals, but there are numerous medics who recommend a place that would do it. They are ready to reveal a fetus's sex for as little as 500 rupees [about eight US dollars]. Doing so is illegal, and discouraged by various campaigns, but the law alone is almost impossible to enforce. Slapping the father on the back and saying "you're a lucky man" is hint enough.

A skewed sex ratio may instead be making the lot of women worse. Robbery, rape and bride trafficking tend to increase in any society with large groups of young single men. And men higher-up the social ladder find wives more easily than those lower-down, the social problems of bachelorhood tend to accumulate like silt among the poorest people and the lowest castes [classes in India]. This is unjust as well as damaging. Moreover, there are reports of unknown numbers of girls who are drugged, beaten and sometimes killed by traffickers. Others, willingly or not, are brought across India's borders, notably from Bangladesh and Myanmar. "Put bluntly, it's a competition over scarce women. Women in India are sometimes permitted, even encouraged, to "marry up" into a higher income bracket or caste, so richer men find it easier to get a bride. The poor are forced into a long or permanent bachelorhood; a status widely frowned upon in India, where marriage is deemed essential to becoming a full member of society. Poor bachelors are often victims of violent crime.

Moreover, the ten-year census may not capture what has been happening recently. For that, go to the sample surveys that India carries out more often. These show a different pattern. The figures are not strictly comparable, because sample surveys show the sex ratio at birth, whereas the census gives it among infants up to the age of six. Still, it is significant the sex ratio at birth is improving, not worsening. In 2003–05 the figure was 880 girls born per 1,000 boys. In 2004–06, that had risen to 892 and in 2006–08, to 904. It is not clear why this should be. The samples could be misleading. But perhaps they reveal a recent change in Indian attitudes towards the value of daughters.

Reasons for Hope

The fears about India's sex ratio are not merely of the harm that today's level will cause when children become adults. People also worry that the ratio will get ever worse, deteriorating towards Chinese levels (which are even more extreme: on a comparable basis, China's sex ratio at birth is about 833 [girls to 1,000 boys]). This fear may be exaggerated. Not only are there signs of an incipient national turnaround, but regional figures give further reasons for hope. The states with the worst ratios, Haryana and Punjab, seem to have had skewed ratios for decades, going back to the 1880s. They now show some of the biggest improvements.

The national average is worsening thanks to states which once were more neutral with regard to sex, such as Tamil Nadu and Orissa; but because they have not had the historical experience of a strong preference for sons. They also seem less likely to push the sex ratio to the extremes that it reached in Punjab or China. If so, the next census in 2021 could show the beginnings of a shift towards normality. The deterioration in north-east and central India may not mark the start of a fresh erosion in the value of Indian girls.

India bans ultrasound scans from being used merely to identify a fetus's sex; it also makes sex selective abortions illegal. But gendercide cannot be reduced just by coercive laws. In middle income places, ultrasound scans are becoming basic prenatal procedures; it is all but impossible to stop parents from getting to know their child's sex. If a government cracks down on legal abortions, families will get illegal ones—risking the life of the mother, as well as that of her unborn daughter. Far more effective would be to persuade parents that their daughters are worth as much as their sons. Changing social attitudes is a difficult thing for governments to do; but ensuring that girls get their fair share of education, and women their fair share of health care, would be a start.

A Security Issue

Many Western countries portrayed India as Asia's great hope, and India's growth as a global power will counter balance China's rise and ensure that rise remains peaceful. Indeed, the U.S. has identified India as a crucial partner for the coming century, and as part of its effort to cultivate a strategic partnership with New Delhi, Washington has even pledged to help India develop its nuclear energy capabilities. But the continued disappearance of India's women and girls is putting the future of India's security partnership with the West at risk. Even in March 2010; U.S. Secretary of State Hillary Clinton stated that "the subjugation of women is a direct threat to the security of the United States." In fact, the security of states is closely linked to the security of women. If Clinton is right, then shouldn't India's dismal female-to-male ratio raise a red flag for American foreign policy?

The most important interventions India could make are improving the economic situation of women and providing a real old-age pension for families that choose to raise daughters.

Regarding the first objective, enforcement of land and property rights for women would go a long way toward erasing the idea that daughters are economically unproductive. Old-age pensions for families with daughters would then complete that circle, tangibly demonstrating that an investment in girls pays off not just for the larger society, but first and foremost for her natal family. Why so few physicians have been tried under India's laws making sex-selective abortion illegal? The Convention on the Elimination of All Forms of Discrimination against Women (CEDAW) gives the international community the right to hold India accountable for the enforcement, or lack of enforcement, of its laws in this regard. India's future will not be brighter for having sunk to 914 girls per 1,000 boys. The daughter deficit will create a society that is much less stable and much more volatile than it would be with a more balanced ratio. The sustainability of peace and stability—for India and the region—will be progressively undermined in lockstep with the devaluation of India's daughters.

"Because of the scarcity of women in China due to the impact of the One-Child Policy . . . domestic trafficking is one of the leading problems in China today."

Gendercide of Girls in China Has Driven the Growth of Sex Trafficking

Susan Tiefenbrun and Christie J. Edwards

Susan Tiefenbrun is a professor at the Thomas Jefferson School of Law in San Diego, California, and Christie J. Edwards, a graduate of Thomas Jefferson, is cochair of the Women in International Law Interest Group. In the following viewpoint, they argue that China has an increasing problem with the kidnapping and sex trafficking of women. They argue that this is related to China's one-child policy, which has resulted in sex-selective abortion and decreasing numbers of women. With a high demand for women as sex partners and wives, the market for trafficked women has boomed. They conclude that China must do more to prosecute traffickers and must eliminate the one-child policy that has helped to fuel the boom in trafficking.

As you read, consider the following questions:

1. What is the typical age of an abducted woman in China, according to Tiefenbrun and Edwards?

2. Why does the one-child policy result in the trafficking of infant girls, according to the authors?

3. What evidence do the authors give to suggest that when countries have low ratios of women to men, the social status of women tends to fall?

According to the 2008 U.S. State Department Trafficking in Persons (TIP) Report, China remains "a source, transit, and destination country for men, women and children trafficked for the purposes of sexual exploitation and forced labor." . . . Some of the factors impeding progress in China's anti-trafficking efforts include "tight controls over civil society organizations, restricted access of foreign anti-trafficking organizations, and the government's systematic lack of transparency," as well as its failure to "address labor trafficking or male victims of sex trafficking."

Because of the scarcity of women in China due to the impact of the One-Child Policy and the force of the male-child preference, domestic trafficking is one of the leading problems in China today. In 2007, the TIP Report stated that there are "an estimated minimum of 10,000 to 20,000 victims trafficked internally per year." The profit earned in human trafficking in China is more than US$7 billion annually, more than arms trafficking or drug trafficking. International organizations state that ninety percent of the trafficking victims are women and children from the Anhui, Guizhou, Henan, Hunan, Sichuan, and Yunnan Provinces who are sent to wealthier provinces in the East and trafficked primarily for sexual exploitation.

The abducted women are usually between the ages of thirteen and twenty-four. While many women are sold into forced and exploitative prostitution, most are purchased as brides in rural parts of China. As the number of available women decreases and the number of peasant families moving to urban areas for jobs increases, peasant men look to traffickers to supply them with a wife. Some say it is economically cheaper to purchase a wife than to pay for a wedding and dowry gifts. Local villagers often sympathize with the husband whose bride tries to escape, and villagers sometimes will return the purchased wife to her husband even if she complains of abuse.

International Trafficking and China

International trafficking of Chinese citizens to Africa, Asia, Europe, Latin America, the Middle East, and North America is increasing. Many poor Chinese women are duped by false promises of legitimate jobs in Taiwan, Thailand, Malaysia, and Japan, only to be sold into prostitution upon their arrival. Although trafficking remains illegal in China, this crime is inadequately enforced, especially in the vulnerable southern provinces near Thailand and Taiwan. In relation to the number of women and children trafficked in China, there are relatively few investigations of trafficking and even fewer trials or convictions. In 2006, Anhui Province, one of the major sources of trafficking victims, only six traffickers were reported convicted and sentenced to life imprisonment. In 2007, China did not report any country-wide conviction records for trafficking.

In 2007, the Chinese government "reported investigating 2375 cases of trafficking of women and children ..., which is significantly lower than the 3371 cases it cited in 2006." These figures are likely based on China's definition of the term "trafficking," which "does not include acts of forced labor, debt bondage, coercion, or involuntary servitude, or offenses committed against male victims." Although China "sustained its record of criminal law enforcement against traffickers," the U.S. State Department reports that these government statistics are difficult to verify. Finally, in 2007, "Chinese law enforcement authorities arrested and punished some traffickers involved in forced labor practices and commercial sexual exploitation, but did not provide data on prosecutions, convictions, or sentences." The lack of transparency in the Chinese judicial system exacerbates the problem of data verification.

Trafficking is not only limited to women and children but also includes infant girls. In poor rural districts of China, the preference for male children is high, and family planning rules are strictly enforced. The One-Child Policy limits the number of children that women may bear, and many women prefer to sell their infant daughter for relatively large sums of money in order to try again for a son. Many women are afraid of the social stigma as well as large fines and penalties imposed on them for violating the one-child limit. While many families are willing to pay the fines if a son is born, most "would never pay that kind of fine for a daughter." The trafficked infant girls are often sold to childless urban parents or rural farmers who desire a girl to help with the housework. Some girls in China are even raised to be child brides for farmers in remote villages. . . .

A Shortage of Women

The Chinese vernacular for young adult males who will never marry is *guang gun-er*, or "bare branches"—those who will never marry because they cannot find spouses. Scholars across a wide array of social sciences, including anthropology, biology, criminology, psychology, organization behavior, and sociology, agree that large numbers of bare branches lead to increased instability, violence, and a potential threat to Chinese society. Bare branches tend to share similar characteristics: they belong primarily to the lowest socioeconomic class; they are likely to be underemployed or unemployed; they are typically transient with few ties to the communities where they work; and they live with other bare branches, creating a distinctive bachelor subculture.

International Trafficking

After China globalized its economy and improved its trade with bordering countries, the human trafficking became internationalized. In November 2008, police in southeastern Fujian province investigated a cross-border trafficking case in which 18 Vietnamese women were brought from Vietnam and sent to China's border provinces, including Yunnan and Guangxi, and were reportedly sold into marriages in rural communities for 20,000 to 30,000 yuan RMB (approximately $3,000–4,400) each. In southwestern Guizhou province, state media reported that courts heard a case involving 30 suspects accused of trafficking more than 80 women over a four-year period from Guizhou to Shanxi, Fujian, Zhejiang, and other eastern provinces. The women were led to believe they were being provided employment, but instead were unwillingly moved to rural areas for forced marriages. Some international rights groups have concluded that China's trafficking problems partially result from the country's social stratification and family planning policy—the "one-child policy."

Xiaobing Li, Civil Liberties in China, *2010.*

In a speech on the demographic crisis in China, Li Weixiong, an advisor to China's political consultative conference on population issues, states that "[s]uch serious gender disproportion poses a major threat to the healthy, harmonious and sustainable growth of the nation's population and would trigger such crimes and social problems as abduction of women and prostitution." An official magazine entitled "Theory and Time," published in Shenyang, China, predicts that the disproportionate gender balance will lead to "a large army of bachelors composed of 90 million men" as well as a severe break-down in social order and the abduction and sale of women. Other scholars agree that as Chinese families consciously se-lect male children over female children, there "will be a sig-nificant increase in societal, and possibly intersocietal, vio-lence"—a terrifying prospect for an elite governing class.

In addition to the high probability of civil unrest, the con-sequences for women in high sex-ratio countries are dire and typically cause their already low societal status to decline fur-ther. "[T]heir levels of literacy and labor-force participation are low," and "[t]heir suicide rate, relative to men's, is also high." Women are also more likely to be kidnapped or sold. "From 1991 through 1996, Chinese police freed 88,000 kid-napped women and children and arrested 143,000 people for participating in the slave trade." In a major campaign against human trafficking in 2000, police claim to have rescued 100,000 women and children, in addition to breaking up kid-napping gangs. These figures are viewed as conservative since law enforcement agencies face large obstacles when trying to enforce the kidnapping and slavery laws. Moreover, there is strong community support of men who buy kidnapped women.

The black market trade in infants, especially girls, has in-creased dramatically due to the desire of some childless couples to have a daughter. The growing sex trade and the in-creased popularity of foreign adoptions has caused some or-phanages to buy healthy children from parents or traffickers. High sex-ratio societies usually have higher levels of prostitu-tion. During the 1990s, an increased number of brothels was reported, servicing mainly urban areas populated by unmar-ried migrant workers. . . .

A Miracle Is Needed

Failures in China's One-Child Policy, the inadequate enforce-ment of Chinese laws protecting women, and the longstanding cultural preference for males have led to discrimination against women and an increase in forced prostitution and trafficking in China. Millions of women are missing in China because of female child abandonment and infanticide. The scarcity of women has resulted in a major increase in the trafficking and sale of foreign women into China. As China shifted from a planned economy to a market economy in 1979, the price of women in China increased in accordance with the market economy principle of supply and demand. The One-Child Policy has caused women to become a high cost commodity.

In order to reverse the deleterious effects of the One-Child Policy and its commodification of women, the Chinese government must make a commitment to implement laws and policies that can reverse longstanding cultural trends and combat discriminatory traditions against women. Civil rights laws enacted in the United States in the 1960s have had a profoundly ameliorative affect on reducing discrimination against African-Americans in American society. There is no reason why the adoption and strict enforcement of Chinese civil rights and trafficking laws could not similarly result in profound cultural change and equality for women in a traditionally male-dominated society now in transition. Since 1979, China has instituted economic reform policies that miraculously work in harmony with a Communist political system. Now China needs to perform another miracle: the adoption of cultural reforms that produce gender parity and that stop the marginalization of women in Chinese society. Only then will the lucrative business of trafficking in women be reduced, if not eliminated entirely.

| "The world-wide phenomenon of human trafficking is a myth."

Worldwide Human Trafficking Is a Myth

Zbigniew Dumienski

As of this writing, Zbigniew Dumienski was pursuing a PhD in political studies at the University of Auckland, New Zealand; he has worked as a research analyst at Nanyang Technological University in Singapore. In the following viewpoint, he argues that trafficking for sex slavery in Asia, China, and worldwide is a myth. He argues that "victims" of trafficking are usually voluntary migrants, who experience harsh conditions but are not best understood as victims. He says that the needs of migrants are ignored and laws regarding migrants distorted by the myth of worldwide human trafficking.

As you read, consider the following questions:

1. What does Dumienski say white slavery came to mean?

2. What crimes does the author argue are often lumped together under the category of "trafficking"?

Zbigniew Dumienski, "Myth and Reality of Human Trafficking: A View from Southeast Asia," *Interdisciplinary Political Studies*, vol. 2, no. 1, March 2012. Copyright © 2012 by Zbigniew Dumienski. All rights reserved. Reproduced by permission.

3. Who are the only trafficking victims who have used the help of rescuers in Myanmar, according to Dumienski?

Human trafficking is commonly seen as a heinous transnational crime affecting millions of migrants from all parts of the globe. According to the US government there are as many as 12.3 million victims of human trafficking worldwide and trafficking is a tremendous, multi-billion-dollar business run by both small networks of traffickers and, increasingly, by "large polycrime international criminal organizations." One could say that these are very alarming developments and that the authors of the preceding claims should be thanked and congratulated for bringing them so forcibly to public attention. The only problem is that it is difficult to find evidence that any of the above is true. More nuanced research that reveals the complexity of the phenomenon of human trafficking is necessary. This article is an attempt to critically evaluate the concept of human trafficking and highlight the challenges and limitations of anti-trafficking campaigns. A critical perspective on these issues is both timely and needed, as more and more funds and energy are invested in this worldwide struggle.

The main argument of this article is that the monolithic crime of human trafficking is largely a myth that has developed with the actual or perceived increase of transnational movements of people from various poorer parts of the globe. A myth does not mean that something is false, instead it is seen as a "collective belief that simplifies reality" [according to researcher Jo Doezema]. By highlighting various problems of both the human trafficking discourse and of anti-trafficking campaigns, this article demonstrates that the discourse on human trafficking fits well into the "myth" category that distorts proper understanding of the problem and has hampered efforts to combat it. More careful research reveals that the story is far from simple, and that the concept of trafficking is highly problematic. Similarly, anti-trafficking efforts, while probably well-meaning, can be detrimental to the interests of the migrants. This article highlights several misconceptions of human trafficking by looking at the problem both from a global perspective and by presenting cases of human trafficking in the Democratic Republic of Timor (East Timor). In addition to a critique of current approaches, it suggests an alternative way of looking at the challenges faced by migrants.

The Myth of White Slavery

The current campaign against human trafficking may seem novel and at its rather early stage, but it is worth remembering that this is not the first time an international movement seeks to eradicate human trafficking. Over a century ago, various transnational moral entrepreneurs together with governments made tremendous efforts in Europe and America to spread awareness about and eliminate what they called "white slavery". Even though discourse on "white slavery" was perhaps never consistent, it nevertheless came to generally mean "the procurement, by force, deceit, or drugs, of a white woman or girl against her will, for prostitution" [according to Doezema]. While some reformers used the language of slavery to depict all types of sex-related jobs, white slavery was above all presented as a phenomenon taking place across borders and as such presumably requiring a strong international response. And indeed, the popular image of "young women driven by poverty, lured by trickery, and compelled by force to prostitution in foreign lands" proved to be so powerful that it led to the creation of a global regime against "white slavery" [according to researchers P. Andreas and E. Nadelmann].

From New York to Australia, countless organizations emerged to rescue women. Furthermore, governments from across the Western world introduced legislation preventing women from travelling. That period saw a real flood of transnational initiatives aimed at suppressing trafficking. Indeed, an unprecedented number of international agreements were signed. These included: the International Agreement for the Suppression of the White Slave Traffic (1904); International Convention for the Suppression of White Slave Traffic (1910); International Convention for the Suppression of the Traffic in Women and Children (1921); International Convention for the Suppression of the Traffic in Women of Full Age (1933).

The interest in white slavery almost completely disappeared with the outbreak of World War II and until relatively recently the image of trafficked women had been absent from public imagination. This does not mean that there were suddenly fewer traffickers, but rather that white slavery/pre-war trafficking had always been a myth that became dissolved by the changes in the post-war social, economic and demographic conditions. Indeed, contemporary historians seem to agree white slavery was largely a myth "triggered by the increase in female migration, including the migration of female prostitutes that was made possible by the increased mobility of populations" [as per researcher F. David]. And it comes as no surprise that restrictions on travelling introduced after both world wars led to the disappearance of the white slavery scare.

The Discourse on Human Trafficking

The recent revival of the trafficking discourse (loaded with sky-is-falling hypotheses) coincided with the collapse of the Iron Curtain [following the end of the Cold War around 1990], and subsequent increase of movement of people to the West from the former Eastern bloc. As it was observed by [researcher N.] Davies, soon after the flats of Western capitals became flooded with young women from Eastern Europe, there were rumours and media reports that led to the creation of a new moral panic—this time bearing the name of human trafficking. And just like a century ago, that panic has fuelled the creation of a specific global regime, narrative, specialist language and institutions.

According to the common narrative, contemporary human trafficking is nothing short of modern slavery, which reduces people to commodities, deprives them of their human rights and freedoms; promotes social breakdown; fuels organized crime; deprives countries of human capital; undermines public health; subverts government authority; and imposes enormous economic costs. The US Department of State, which seems to be leading the global struggle against trafficking, believes the number of people trafficked across national borders annually to be anywhere between 600,000–800,000 people. The International Labour Organization (ILO) on the other hand provided an estimate of the number of trafficked victims at any given time to be 2.45 million. Just like in the 19th century, the transnational character of the human trafficking story means that any effort of combating human trafficking must by definition be made at all levels—i.e. national, regional, and global. The most recent global effort to address this crime resulted in the adoption of the Protocol to Prevent, Suppress and Punish Trafficking in Persons, Especially Women and Children, supplementing the UN Convention against Transnational Organized Crime on 25 December 2003. The Protocol that for the first time provided a universally agreed upon definition of trafficking in persons further inflated a world-wide interest in the issue of trafficking. But it was because of the unilateral action undertaken by the US that human trafficking became one of the most popular and fashionable social causes. The US Administration's Trafficking in Persons Report is advertised (by the United States) as the most comprehensive worldwide report on the efforts of governments to combat severe forms of trafficking in persons. Ever since the publication of its first issue, it has served as a diplomatic tool used by the US government to compel countries from across the globe to adopt and comply with presumably the only right standards promoted by the American administration.

Southeast Asia is one of the major sources of human trafficking. Interests in human trafficking in Southeast Asia have their origins in the growing concerns for irregular migration and the sex industry. One of the earliest attempts to address the reportedly growing phenomenon of human trafficking was the Bangkok Declaration on Irregular Migration of April 1999. The declaration observed that "international migration, particularly irregular migration, has increasingly become a major economic, social, humanitarian, political and security concern". The declaration also recognised the allegedly "increasing activities of transnational organized criminal groups and others that profit from smuggling of and trafficking in human beings, especially women and children" and called for "comprehensive, coherent and effective policies on irregular/undocumented migration" to combat human trafficking. According to one popular estimate, 200,000–250,000 women and children are trafficked each year from the region. Such impressive estimates of cases of trafficking in Southeast Asia have led to increased attention being paid to human trafficking in the region. The Association of Southeast Asian Nations (ASEAN) went as far as to even claim that the phenomenon of human trafficking is now so serious that it presents a significant challenge to the creation of a "prosperous and peaceful community" in Southeast Asia—a bold statement, for an organization composed to a significant degree of countries already facing such challenges as extreme poverty, corruption, organized violence and environmental degradation.

As a result of the Bangkok Declaration of 1999 and the adoption of the UN Trafficking Protocol in 2003, there have been many highly publicised developments in the fight against trafficking in Southeast Asia spearheaded by ASEAN. The key commitments of ASEAN Member Countries regarding trafficking in persons are contained today in legal instruments such as the 1997 ASEAN Declaration on Transnational Crime and the 2004 ASEAN Declaration against Trafficking in Persons, Particularly Women and Children.

"Fishy" Numbers

As [researchers P.] Andreas and [K.] Greenhill once observed, "in practical political terms, if something is not measured it does not exist, if it is not counted it does not count." This reality has certainly been recognized by the US TIP Report 2010, which presents figures on the estimated number of victims worldwide and the number of people experiencing forced labour in North Korea—150,000–200,000, which is remarkable intelligence on a country that is considered an impenetrable "intelligence nightmare". Journalists too like to use big numbers to inform the public about the alleged scale of trafficking. For instance, every new major sports event attracts dramatic news stories (of very dubious merit) on the "thousands" of victims of human trafficking. . . .

What all these figures have in common is that they rarely have identifiable sources or transparent methodologies behind them. In most instances, they are nothing more than the "result of certain activists who pull their numbers out of thin air" [as researcher C. Bialik put it]. These estimates are oftentimes so tenuous that debunking them has become "a sport for sceptical journalists" [as writer K. Howley put it]. The truth is that all attempts to quantify human trafficking are [as researcher L. Agustin stated in 2008] "questionable" since the phenomenon of trafficking is reportedly a vague "covert activity happening in the shadow economy" [according to N. Rothschild]. What statistics on human trafficking seem to do best is to obscure the murkiness of the concept itself.

Crime or Crimes?

Human trafficking is usually seen as a monolithic crime, but this notion can be misleading. Ultimately, this "single big crime" is a composite category that lumps together actions that are distinct in nature—some of them can involve force or fraud, and some of them can be based on consent; some of them have easily identifiable victims, and some do not; some involve such offences as forgery or smuggling, and some are based on the use of perfectly legitimate documents and channels of transportation. Hence, what is commonly understood as the single big crime of human trafficking is any act of migration (mainly illegal) that involves some crimes (and sometimes a mere possibility of crimes) against the migrant.

At first sight, this seems fair and logical. However, if particular crimes can be readily identified, why is there a need for a new, all-encompassing (and vague) category of a single big crime? The problem with the single-big-crime approach is twofold. First, not all elements of the complex process of illegal migration are of a criminal or coercive nature. It is difficult to see how it could be helpful to the migrant to criminalize the whole process of migration just because some elements of the process involve coercion.

Second, not everything that might seem coercive or abusive is considered as such by the migrant. This is especially true in the case of illegal migration, which is a complex phenomenon that always involves some elements that could be considered criminal or coercive. For instance, "would-be travellers commonly seek help from intermediaries (. . .) who sell information, services and documents. When travellers cannot afford to buy these outright, they go into debt" [according to Agustin]. These debts must be paid back, often on very harsh terms, yet in most instances, they were incurred voluntarily. Similarly, being forced to work might mean many different things. In the context of the sex industry, "some people feel forced who could physically escape" (Agustin). Others might feel forced because it is the best or the only choice available to them. Even in cases of actual violence (or threats of it), it is not clear why existing laws would not be sufficient to deal with the perpetrator of the violent act. Moreover, rather than introducing tougher criminalization what is necessary is to provide assistance to migrants to avoid violence that often accompanies illegal migration.

The only possible rationale for the creation of a unified crime of "human trafficking" seems to be that it may perhaps allow the illegal migrant not to be treated as a criminal (which could have been achieved simply by easing migration regulations). This proposition is underpinned by a strange logic—a helpless victim should be rewarded with no criminal charges, and perhaps even legal status, while an able-bodied and successful, but illegal, economic migrant would continue to be punished and persecuted as a criminal. Despite the above problems, the most dominant feature of anti-trafficking campaigns is a broad approach to illegal migration that may involve some form of what campaigners would define as abuse or coercion. The result is that "efforts to prevent 'trafficking' often try to prevent migration itself" (Agustin). In many instances, anti-traffickers seek to identify people in danger of experiencing abuse and try to prevent them from undertaking a risky migration. The possibility that some people may actually take the risks is not taken into consideration. This leads to the most fundamental problem with the current human trafficking discourse—the belief that illegal migrants do not necessarily have free will.

The "Rescue Industry"

Today there are hundreds of NGOs [nongovernmental organizations] worldwide, particularly in Southeast Asia, working on "rescuing" victims of human trafficking. In addition to running shelters, they advocate new anti-trafficking legislation and assist law enforcement agencies on rescue missions (raids). They are perhaps the most visible manifestation of the tendency to view migrants as pathetic victims who need to be saved.

While this all might sound good and noble, the reality is that in many instances the greatest opponents of the rescuers are not some evil traffickers but the alleged victims. Rescue raids everywhere from the UK to Cambodia have not only failed to find any perpetrators or victims but have also demonstrated that "the anti-trafficking industry can cause harm and distress to migrant families, undermine global freedom of movement, and warp the public's perception of immigration" [according to *Spiked* editor Brendan O'Neill]. This is not to suggest that migrants do not require help, or that they do not experience abuse, but rather that in most cases they do not necessarily need to be rescued. Migrants are not passive objects and have often demonstrated a striking capacity to fight against abuses or exploitation. In one instance, a group of Thai migrants approached their embassy in Madrid to complain about being forced into working as prostitutes [according to the *Bangkok Post* in 2010].

However, the lack of evidence of large-scale trafficking requiring rescue missions does not necessarily make anti-traffickers reconsider their position. Rather, this is used to put forward a more sinister scenario in which women fail to identify themselves as victims and their employers as traffickers either because they are suffering from some Stockholm Syndrome-style[1] psychological disorder or because they are lying. This is a terrifying logic that effectively suggests that no evidence of oppression should be seen as evidence of particularly severe oppression. One is free to imagine where such thinking can lead.

Demystifying Trafficking in East Timor

Timor-Leste [East Timor] is a small, young and extremely poor Southeast Asian country. Yet, despite its underdevelopment, it has been reported as a destination country for human traffickers. Allegedly, women are being trafficked from South East Asian countries into East Timor to work as sex slaves for local men and "wealthy and salacious UN and other foreign workers" [as reported by ABC News in 2003]. These claims

1. Stockholm Syndrome is a psychological phenomenon in which hostages express sympathy for or identify with their kidnappers.

sound very alarming. However, a closer look at the situation of migrants in Timor-Leste reveals that the stories of slaves and victims are largely founded on the kind of misunderstandings and prejudices highlighted in the previous sections of this article.

So far, the most comprehensive report on human trafficking in Timor-Leste is one from a local non-governmental organization Alola Foundation. The report prefers the term "sex workers" rather than sex slaves and insists on the decriminalization of sex workers that should not be treated as criminals. However, the report's judgment on trafficking suffers from several limitations. First, while Alola argues for not treating sex workers as potential criminals, they do not hesitate to see them all as potential victims of elaborate trafficking schemes. For instance, while the authors of the report admit to having failed to collect any significant data on sex workers from China, who reportedly form the second largest group of foreign sex workers, they write that all of them should be seen as potential trafficking victims. Why 100 per cent of them should not instead be seen [as] regular economic migrants is not clear. Second, to be forced is interpreted quite loosely. For instance, a person responsible for coordinating the anti-trafficking efforts at the Alola Foundation explained to the author of this article that "traffickers forced Chinese girls to work as prostitutes by taking their passports away." The withholding of passports alone cannot be seen as enslavement, especially since the Chinese embassy is among the most visible buildings in [the capital city of] Dili.

The Alola Foundation admits that since they started their work on the topic a few years ago, there have only been a handful of cases in which foreign women have been subjected to violence, manipulation and coercion. At the same time, Alola Foundation staff agreed that in all those cases, the abuse had much more to do with the illegality and underground character of brothels than with the process of migration per se.

The UN rejects the media stories about its staff using the services of sex slaves. According to the UN Integrated Mission in Timor-Leste's (UNMIT) spokesman, Gyorgy Kakuk, UN personnel are in fact strictly prohibited from using any type of sex services. In fact, several aid workers also observed that the foreign soldiers do not need to go to brothels to have sex, as the vast majority of aid workers in Dili are single females who too have sexual needs. And even if, despite the above, some soldiers might decide to pay for sex, there is no reason why this should be accompanied by violence or abuse.

According to the data retrieved from the interviews, foreigners in the sex industry in Timor-Leste can make good money by catering to the needs of foreign workers or by serving the wealthier locals. The biggest problem they face is not human trafficking, but the illegality of the organized sex industry and the associated brutal and humiliating police rescue raids. While the focus of anti-traffickers is on the sex industry—with the IOM [International Organization for Migration] and a local non-governmental organization Psychosocial Recovery & Development in East Timor (PRADET), jointly establishing a shelter for "trafficked women and girls" [according to the US State Department]—so far the only victims using the help of the rescuers have been a few fishermen from Myanmar who claim to have been kept as forced labour on the foreign fishing vessels from which they had managed to escape by swimming to the shores of Timor-Leste when the boats happened to be passing by. As tragic as their story is, this is hardly an example of human trafficking to Timor-Leste.

There is simply no sufficient evidence that there are networks of traffickers in Timor-Leste. However, yet again, a lack of evidence has been taken as proof that a problem exists. Apparently, either the traffickers are very sophisticated or the Timorese criminal justice system very inefficient at recording traffickers. With such an approach, one can only expect a rise in the trafficking warnings coming from Dili.

A Scare Story

Illegal migration is risky. Many who undertake it experience abuse, mistreatment and live in fear. Illegal migrants usually have little choice but to accept what many in the developed world would consider humiliating or inhumane jobs. Certainly, these migrants would welcome more rights and protection. Yet, the current anti-trafficking hype—and the associated depoliticizing of debates on migration—can hardly make their situation better. The problem faced by the vast majority of illegal migrants is not that they can be sold like cattle, but rather that with legal migration denied to them, they must take many more risks than they would prefer. While abuse is real, the world-wide phenomenon of human trafficking is a myth that in many ways resembles its historical precedent, the white slavery panic that became prominent a century ago. Contemporary trafficking myth is an exciting, almost pornographic, yet ultimately very simplistic and racist story of helpless Third World women and children, ruthless Oriental or Eastern European men and noble Western rescuers. And just like any other contemporary scare story, it leads to unnecessary expenditure, insensible and illiberal legislation, and unreasonable actions.

In Timor-Leste illegal migrants are rarely, if ever, seen as individuals with agency who may require solidarity and advocacy. Instead, they are either seen as criminals or as hapless victims who need to be rescued and sheltered. While the former is probably worse for migrants than the latter, neither of these approaches effectively deals with the problems experienced by illegal migrants and sex workers. In order to alleviate the situation, the public and governments should realise the direct link between the abuses they so firmly stand against and the fact that quite a few people work, live and travel in an illegal and underground manner. This is not to suggest that those opposing abuse must necessarily support absolute freedom of migration and legality of all types of employment. At the very minimum, however, they should try to address abuses regardless of the victims' immigration or employment status. One does not need to invent human trafficking to investigate and prosecute such crimes as kidnapping, beating, raping or threatening. On the contrary, targeting specific crimes, rather than some abstract composite category could not only be easier, but also more in line with migrants' wishes and interests. Furthermore, it could bring more transparency, justice, clarity and accountability to law enforcement and the protection of victims. For now, the struggle against over-hyped, yet murky human trafficking is carried out with little accountability and self-reflection. Indeed, it is difficult to imagine how efforts against trafficking could be accountable, clear or even reasonable if they focus on a set of highly controversial and vague concepts, lack any reliable statistics, often deny agency to victims, and go across borders with little or no cultural sensitivity. What is needed today not only in Timor-Leste, but also in the ASEAN region and elsewhere, is a serious debate on the rights of migrants and sex workers. Hopefully, the current moral furore over trafficking will not make this impossible.

Periodical and Internet Sources Bibliography

The following articles have been selected to supplement the diverse views presented in this chapter.

All Girls Allowed	"Gendercide Statistics," n.d. www.allgirlsallowed.org.
The Economist	"India's Skewed Sex Ratios: Gendercide Stings," December 18, 2012.
Beverly Hill	"Beverly Hill: Let's End the Invisible Slaughter of Women," Gendercide Awareness Project, January 15, 2013. http://gendap.org.
Toura Izri	"*It's a Girl* Documentary Explores Gendercide in China and India," *The Star* (Toronto), November 14, 2012.
Walter Russell Mead	"India's Gendercide Doesn't Stop at Birth," *The Feed* (blog), *American Interest*, January 31, 2012. www.the-american-interest.com/blog.
Allison Pearson	"In the Third World. Unwanted Baby Girls 'Disappear.' It's Called Gendercide. And It's Happening in This Country Too," *Sunday Telegraph* (London), February 24, 2012.
Elizabeth Vargas	"'All Those Little Faces': Elizabeth Vargas Explores India's 'Gendercide,'" ABC News, December 10, 2011. http://abcnews.go.com.
Ronald Weitzer	"Myths About Human Trafficking," *Huffington Post*, August 24, 2011. www.huffingtonpost.com.
Wendy Wright	"UN Agencies Fuel Sex Selective Abortion and the Devaluation of Women," C-FAM, March 8, 2012. www.c-fam.org.

OPPOSING
VIEWPOINTS®
SERIES

What Are Common Practices of Gendercide in Developed Countries?

Chapter Preface

Sex-selective abortion is usually seen as an issue particularly affecting Asian nations like China and India. However, some parts of Europe also have problems with sex-selective abortions and gendercide.

In particular, there is evidence of widespread son selection in the Caucasus—namely, the nations of Armenia, Azerbaijan, and Georgia. Under normal conditions, 105 boys are born for every 100 girls. This was the ratio in the Caucasus until 1991, when those nations that had been part of the Soviet Union became independent. Since then, gender ratios have gone out of balance. In Armenia and Azerbaijan, 112 boys are born for every 100 girls; in Georgia it is 111 boys for every 100 girls.

The preference for sons in the Caucasus has similar roots to son preference in other areas. Daughters in the Caucasus generally leave home to go to their husband's family. Sons are expected to take care of their parents in old age. Families thus have a strong incentive to have at least one son. As one Armenian man told Parandzem Hovhannisyan and Aliya Haqverdi in a September 30, 2011, article at the Institute for War and Peace Reporting, "An Armenian family isn't complete unless there's an heir to carry on the name."

In response to the situation in the Caucasus, the Parliamentary Assembly of the Council of Europe (PACE) denounced sex-selective abortion and the pressures that lead families to abort their daughters. PACE has no legal authority but is influential in establishing international law. The Swedish originator of the resolution, Doris Stump, said that the resolution attempted to balance abortion rights with the need to restrict sex-selective abortions. "It touches on an area that we do not want to question: the right to have an abortion in countries where they have that," Stump was quoted as saying in a November 10, 2011, article by Hilary White at LifeSite-

News. "At the same time," she added, "everyone accepts that there is a problem in our societies with sex selection, or we could have a problem if we go on like this."

The call for a ban on sex-selective abortion has been controversial. Some doctors and medical professionals in the Caucasus worry that limiting legal abortion will cause women to risk their health by seeking out illegal practitioners. On the other hand, some critics argue that the resolution should call for a ban not just on sex-selective abortions but on abortions of those with genetic diseases or disabilities.

The viewpoints in this chapter will examine the issue of sex-selective abortion in some Western regions, including the United States, Canada, and Britain.

"Girl babies are 'disappearing' from British Indian families at a rate approaching 100 a year."

British Immigrant Communities Commit Gendercide via Sex-Selective Abortion

Kishwar Desai

Kishwar Desai is an Indian novelist and columnist. In the following viewpoint, she argues that the prejudice against women in India has influenced Indian communities in Britain. She says that Indian women in Britain often abort baby girls or try to use sperm-selection technology to ensure that only boys will be born. She says that the solution must be to raise the status of women in India and eliminate such customs as dowries, so that people do not see daughters as unwanted economic burdens.

As you read, consider the following questions:

1. Why is sperm sorting no longer available in Britain, according to the author?

Kishwar Desai, "Britain's Hidden Gendercide: How Britain's Asians Are Copying Indian Cousins and Aborting Girls," *Daily Mail*, May 11, 2010. Copyright © 2010 by Kishwar Desai. All rights reserved. Reproduced by permission.

2. According to Desai, what is *Kanya Daan*?

3. What does Desai say ensures the passage of prejudice against daughters from generation to generation?

For the hospital sonographer, it's just another routine 20-week ultrasound scan. The baby is developing perfectly and, helpfully, is lying in the right position to make identification of its gender straightforward. 'Would you like to know the sex?' she asks. The anxious-looking Indian woman who has been staring so intently at the monitor, smiles nervously. 'Oh yes, please,' she says, her slight Midlands accent betraying the fact that she was born in Britain.

Disappearing Girls

'Well, you're having a little girl. Isn't that lovely?' If the sonographer had been a little less tired, she might have noticed the slight hesitation before her patient's reply, the fleeting look of desperate disappointment that crossed her face. But both are gone in a split second. 'Oh yes, wonderful news, my husband will be pleased.'

But the woman is lying—just as hundreds of other British women of Indian origin do every year. Their husbands certainly *won't* be pleased by news of another daughter, nor, more often than not, are they.

What was it *daadi* (grandmother) used to say? Bringing up a baby girl is like watering a neighbour's garden. What her grandmother meant, of course, is that it's an absolute waste of time and money.

As she straightens her clothing and walks out of the hospital, the woman shudders, knowing full well what lies ahead. The long flight to India, the noisy taxi ride through the crowded Delhi streets to the clinic, and the pain and horror of a late abortion. But her husband was adamant; they simply could not afford another daughter.

And so, ten days later and despite the fact that abortion on the grounds of gender is technically illegal in India, the life of yet another British Indian baby girl ends on the bloodied operating table of a Delhi abortion clinic before it has even begun. She is killed simply for being a girl.

Having carried out extensive research into the subject for my new novel, I'm convinced that scenarios like this are played out regularly in most of Britain's major cities. Indeed, research from Oxford University has estimated that girl babies are 'disappearing' from British Indian families at a rate approaching 100 a year. As with all official estimates, the reality could well be more.

By 'disappearing', I mean British Indian communities in this country are failing to produce the number of girl babies that science tells us to expect, which, broadly speaking, is 950 girls for every 1,000 boys.

And how are they doing this? By pursuing a determined programme of sex selection, either by aborting female foetuses or, increasingly—particularly among more affluent families—by doing everything in their power to ensure that the fertilised egg implanted in the mother's womb is a male one. This can be done by a technique known as 'sperm sorting'— where sperm carrying the male Y chromosome are separated from those carrying the female X chromosome—or, more reliably, by IVF [in vitro fertilization].

For a few years, such techniques seemed the answer to an awful lot of devout prayers, but in 2007—amid mounting controversy about babies being designed to order—the Human Fertilisation and Embryology Authority outlawed gender selection in this way. Specialist clinics in London, Birmingham and Glasgow which had been offering couples the chance to choose the sex of their babies—and which had been advertising extensively in the Punjabi [Indian] press in Britain—were forced to close.

Percent of Women Who had One or More Previous Abortions by Ethnicity in England and Wales, 2011

Ethnicity	Percent
Asian or Asian British	32%
Black or Black British	49%
Chinese or other ethnic group	33%
Mixed	45%
White	35%
All women	36%

TAKEN FROM: Department of Health (UK), "Abortion Statistics, England and Wales: 2011," May 2012. www.gov.uk.

But the practice goes on, with wealthier British Indian families travelling to the U.S., Europe or indeed to India in their efforts to have a male child.

A Preference for Sons

It is difficult for those of white British origins, who come from a culture where the safe arrival of a healthy baby girl is a cause for celebration, to understand the deep-rooted commitment of British Indian families to what has become known as 'son preference'.

You have to travel to India itself to even try to understand it. For it is only there that you begin to grasp the extraordinary paradox that is modern India.

On the one hand, you have one of the most vibrant and fast-growing economies in the world; on the other, you have a deeply patriarchal society, where women are not just seen as second-class citizens but as potentially ruinous economic liabilities, too.

It seems impossible that the country which gave the world one of its first female prime ministers, Indira Gandhi, and produces an ever-growing number of glamorous, highly paid film stars—such as former Miss World Aishwarya Rai, Bollywood actress Shilpa Shetty and *Slumdog Millionaire* star Freida Pinto—could also be the country where millions of women live a life of degradation and humiliation. But it's true; Indian newspapers are routinely filled with stories of rape, honour killings and domestic violence.

But the worst-kept secret is this preference for sons, an almost visceral need for male progeny that not only transcends class, caste and religion, but which has spread across oceans to every Indian community in the world; Britain's, of course, included.

When I was born many moons ago in Ambala in Northern India, I was fortunate that my parents were delighted by my arrival; they'd wanted a daughter.

But other relatives were horrified, and my mother remembers being taken to a neighbour's house, where the matriarch was to be found sitting on her daybed. My mother was told firmly that the matriarch had buried six daughters. The visit was supposed to teach her a lesson she would never forget.

It didn't work for my mother, but such harsh lessons have certainly left their mark on millions of other Indian women. Traditionally, unwanted girl babies are fed opium and left to die; others, I'm afraid, meet far nastier ends as India's poor do what they have been doing since before the Raj [British control of India]—murdering their unwanted daughters.

But with abortion available pretty much on demand up to the 20th week (and illegally much later for a price) more affluent Indian women are getting evermore resourceful at using medical science to find out the sex of the baby they are carrying.

If the technician from the mobile ultrasound clinic isn't sure, there's always a corrupt doctor who can carry out an amniocentesis test (which analyses chromosomes) for a price. If the result comes back 'female', the foetus's grim fate is sealed, as the statistics make clear.

In 1991, the child sex ratio was already a depressed 945 girls per 1,000 boys in India—instead of the usual 950. But by 2001 it was down to 927, and in some of the worst regions, such as Punjab and Delhi, it's heading towards 800. One particular hospital in the Punjab has not registered the birth of any baby girls at all.

Estimates vary as to how many Indian women are now 'missing' from the population, but it's thought to be somewhere between ten and 35 million over the past 20 years. Female foeticide, gendercide—call it what you will—it's a terrible and chilling statistic.

By most western standards this is horrific, but in India— and, by extension, in Indian emigrant communities throughout the world—the brutal practice makes sound economic sense.

The Dowry Tradition

It may cost money to bribe a doctor to carry out an illegal sex test and then for the subsequent abortion, but compared with the cost of raising a daughter it's a pittance.

In Britain, the father of the bride symbolically gives away his daughter on her wedding day. But in India, the giving away is literal. We call it *Kanya Daan* and it means that from the day she gets married, an Indian girl—and all her possessions—belongs to her husband's family.

Hand in glove with this goes the tradition of dowry, which more or less died out in Britain with [early nineteenth-century romantic novelist] Jane Austen but is of tremendous importance to Indian families, whether they are in Mumbai [India] or Birmingham [England]. Jewellery, cash, cars, even houses— the value of the dowry an Indian girl's family must pay to the family of her future husband can run to tens of thousands of pounds. Marrying off one daughter can be expensive, but two, three—that can be ruinous.

As a result, Indians remain wedded to the idea of boys being best and girls little more than a liability. Small wonder that Indian families place such importance on marrying off any daughters as quickly as possible.

What is surprising, at least to Western eyes, is that this preference for sons is most actively passed from one generation to the next by the women. A British-Indian friend of mine recently gave birth to a daughter and while there was a younger generation of Indian women like me, keen to celebrate the arrival, we were outnumbered by an older generation of female cousins and aunts, some of whom were in tears at the wretched fate that had befallen my friend. It was as though someone had died, not just been born.

The problem is that educated, emancipated Indian women are the exception, while more traditional women, the sort who sit sobbing over the arrival of an unwanted girl, are the rule. They pass on to the next generation what they have learned from bitter experience: that they are subservient to men; their usually loveless marriages will be arranged for them; and the size of their dowry matters more than their education.

Living in liberal societies such as the UK puts another strain on families: they have to guard the virginities of their daughters from the moment they reach puberty. It's not always possible to do so. For sons, the same pressure does not apply.

Put like that, it's no wonder they greet the birth of a girl with tears.

From India to Britain

And so the tradition passes on from one generation to the next, its passage eased in this country by the fact that if a British Indian girl doesn't marry a British Indian man she tends to marry a man from India itself. So the tie to the mother country—and all its traditions—is constantly renewed, and therefore remains as strong as ever.

I discovered this while doing some research for my new novel, *Witness The Night,* which has sex selection as one of its central themes. Almost everyone I met knew of British Indian families who remain strongly prejudiced in favour of sons.

No one wanted to talk about the highly sensitive subject of abortion on the grounds of gender, but many knew of couples who had gone abroad to pursue the IVF option offered by gender selection clinics.

Daughters are welcomed into some British Indian families, they said, but they will often be treated—at least in terms of education and career opportunities—in a way that is far inferior to their brothers.

Which is yet another reason why I so passionately believe that this wholesale and, at times, lethal oppression of an entire sex cannot be allowed to continue. And given the strengths of the ties between India and its emigrant communities, the solution must lie in India itself.

It's striking that the problems women face in modern India are not dissimilar to the problems women faced in this country a century ago, when primogeniture [the rule of first-born] ensured property passed from father to eldest son, women didn't have the vote and a good marriage was considered more important than a good education.

Thankfully, Indian women do have a vote in the country that remains the world's biggest democracy, although whether they get the chance to use it properly is a distinctly moot point. But real gender equality will require far more radical change.

India's complex inheritance and divorce laws require further reform, but Indian women also have to be given the same economic opportunities their brothers and husbands enjoy.

They need to become economic assets, not liabilities, and the only way of doing that is by ensuring they have equal access to education, jobs and careers.

Recently, I was in Mumbai, the heart of India's booming stock market, and yet in this bustling, metropolitan city the bodies of newborn baby girls were still being washed up on the beach.

It was there, too, that I read a tiny newspaper story about a woman who had three daughters but was under huge pressure from her husband and his family to produce a male child. In desperation and despair, the poor woman took her three unwanted daughters and jumped into a well. She survived, but tragically not her daughters. India's secret gendercide had just claimed another three innocent girls.

"*[The outcry] has nothing to do with sex selection. Rather, it looks like the result of a concerted campaign to smear and discredit abortion providers.*"

Stoking Fears That British Immigrant Communities Commit Gendercide Is Only Aimed at Limiting Abortion

Jennie Bristow

Jennie Bristow is an associate for the Centre for Parenting Culture Studies at the University of Kent and the editor of Abortion Review, *the magazine of the British Pregnancy Advisory Service. In the following viewpoint, Bristow argues that there is little evidence of systemic sex-selective abortion in the UK. She also says that the push to put more restrictions on abortion in order to avoid sex selection is misguided, and violates the UK's commitment to giving primacy to women's choices and mental health in the abortion decision.*

As you read, consider the following questions:

1. According to Bristow, what did the *Daily Telegraph* investigation of pregnancy clinics in Britain find?

Jennie Bristow, "Sex Selection and the Abortion Counseling Conspiracy," *Abortion Review*, May 31, 2012. Copyright © 2012 by Abortion Review. All rights reserved. Reproduced by permission.

2. What was the Dorries Amendment, and what does Bristow say happened to it?

3. What role do Lansley, Milton, and Dorries see for abortion counselors, according to the author?

Are women in Britain flocking to abortion clinics to commit 'gendercide' of female fetuses? Of course they aren't. When the *Daily Telegraph* newspaper, well known for its anti-abortion stance, conducted a sting operation last week [mid-February 2012] designed to uncover the scale of 'sex-selective abortion', its major 'abortion investigation' claimed to find 'some doctors willing to falsify official paperwork to arrange what would be illegal activity'—and 'others who refused to countenance any such request'.

Smearing Abortion Providers

Beneath the overblown hyperbole, what did the investigation actually find? Undercover journalists for the *Telegraph* visited a small number of clinics, of which at least six were run by the charity British Pregnancy Advisory Service (BPAS), requesting an abortion because the fetus was a girl, or in some cases a boy. They were denied an abortion at all of the BPAS clinics, and found three doctors in private practice who indicated that they would arrange the procedure. No abortions actually took place.

Nonetheless, Health Secretary Andrew Lansley wasted no time in declaring that police investigations would follow, and the Chief Medical Officer immediately wrote to all abortion providers to clarify their obligations under the 1967 Abortion Act. A chill has settled over those working in abortion services about the extent to which doctors are given license to interpret the Abortion Act, without falling foul of the misinterpretations of the antics of undercover journalists with a political agenda. As Nadine Dorries, maverick MP [minister of Parliament] for mid-Bedfordshire, crowed in a blog entry on ConservativeHome on 26 February, 'The spotlight is full on abortion practice'.

How can a story like this, which comes out of nowhere and is based on so little, develop so much momentum in the space of a few days? The answer is that this story did not come out of nowhere, and it has nothing to do with sex selection. Rather, it looks like the result of a concerted campaign to smear and discredit abortion providers, in order to pave the way for a politically-motivated reform of the abortion service.

The Dorries Amendment

The *Daily Telegraph* published its sex selection investigation just as a cross-party group of MPs is busily discussing options for changing the way abortion counselling is provided. The call for reform originated from an amendment laid down by Nadine Dorries MP, with Frank Field MP, to the Health and Social Care Bill last year [2011].

Dorries's proposal, to strip abortion providers of the ability to provide women with information, advice and counselling before abortion and to transfer this function to 'independent counsellors', was spectacularly defeated in a Parliamentary debate, by 368 votes to 118. However, during this debate Public Health Minister Anne Milton formally opposed the Dorries amendment and announced the Department of Health's intention to launch a consultation on the question of abortion counselling.

This consultation is currently taking place, and it is likely to result in the creation of an official 'register' of pregnancy counsellors. One result of this may be to open up the commissioning of pregnancy counselling services to organisations beyond the registered Pregnancy Advisory Bureaux, which currently offer this service and refer women for abortions. There has been concern that the new layer of pregnancy counsellors involved in this proposed system may include organisations that have an in-principle objection to abortion; there is also a worry about the consequences for women's speed and ease of access to abortion, if pregnancy counselling is to be provided separately to abortion referral.

Politically, some have raised serious objections to the way that this consultation has proceeded despite the proposal having been debated and categorically rejected by Parliament. The pro-choice MP Diane Abbott went so far as to resign from the consultation group, complaining that the process was a 'stitch-up' [a set-up, or trick].

What has any of this to do with sex selection? Nothing at all. But it is striking that, within a day of the *Telegraph* publishing its investigation, Health Secretary Andrew Lansley wrote an article in that newspaper, arguing:

> Deciding to have an abortion is a life-changing decision. The law makes clear that health professionals need to support women in taking this decision. We will not only uphold that law, but it is why—in discussion with all main parties—we are planning to consult on counselling arrangements for women seeking an abortion. All women seeking an abortion should have the opportunity, if they so choose, to discuss at length and in detail with a professional their decision and the impact it may have. Whatever the outcome of our consultation on counselling, our laws will remain the same unless, and until, Parliament decides otherwise.

This quote is revealing, for a number of reasons. First of all, it links the spurious fears about sex selection with an existing government initiative about abortion counselling, though on the face of it there is no link at all between a doctor's preparedness to 'flout the law', and whether counselling is provided by somebody who also provides abortion or is formally 'independent'.

An Insult to Medical Professionals

Lansley sees a link however, and this is presumably because he has accepted the scurrilous allegations made by Dorries and Field in proposing their abortion counselling amendment to Parliament—that the problem with abortion providers providing pregnancy counselling is that they have a 'vested interest' in encouraging women to have abortions, because they receive fees or NHS [National Health Service] funding to carry out the procedures. Or to put it another way—abortion providers are prepared to terminate pregnancies on the grounds of fetal sex just because they want the money.

Not only is this argument an insult to the professional judgement of the doctors and nurses who work in abortion care, it also makes little sense. Abortion doctors realise that making a fast buck by providing a service that falls outside of the law can carry enormous costs to one's career and reputation. That is why most doctors—and the majority of the clinics that the *Daily Telegraph* tried to 'sting'—operate within the law, even if they disagree with some of its restrictions. For example, many abortion doctors would actually prefer a situation where women were provided with abortions on request, or at least with the approval of one doctor (rather than two, as is currently the case); but they comply with the law nonetheless.

More importantly, those who work in abortion services do not have a desire to terminate pregnancies as might, for example, those who work in cancer services have a desire to eradicate tumours. Abortion doctors recognise that pregnancy is not an illness and that the fetus has a moral status; their commitment to abortion rests on the knowledge of what nurturing the fetus to birth and beyond means to the pregnant woman.

Abortion services exist to enable individual women to act on their choice regarding their pregnancy. This means that it is only in the abortion doctor's interest to terminate a pregnancy if a woman wants it to be terminated, and the doctor feels this is in her interests. The idea that abortion services are on some kind of mission to terminate wanted pregnancies is, quite simply, bizarre. Yet the notion of 'vested interests' encapsulates this idea.

The Counsellor as 'Gatekeeper'

The second aspect of Lansley's quote that deserves attention is the role he ascribes to the abortion counsellor. Noting that 'Deciding to have an abortion is a life-changing decision', he goes on to talk about why women should be able to discuss their decision in detail. Existing arrangements already provide women with that opportunity, should they want it, so what is different about what Lansley is proposing?

The framework to be established by a new, 'independent' abortion counselling structure clearly sees a very different role for counsellors that that which has been historically established. The pregnancy options discussion was incorporated into the abortion service in order to give women the space to work through whether abortion was the right decision for them, and the role of counselling was to ensure that they understood what the procedure entailed and that they were not being somehow coerced into their request.

The role envisaged for pregnancy counselling by Lansley, Milton and Dorries seems to be a rather more structured 'gatekeeping' function, where women are to account for their decisions and, potentially, have these decisions challenged. Why else would abortion counselling be flagged up in relation to a woman's request to abort her fetus on the grounds of its sex, if it were not to indicate the need for someone to tell her why this is a bad reason for seeking abortion?

Here we get into very muddy waters indeed. Fetal sex is not a legal ground for abortion—that is true. But neither is any other 'choice' ground for a woman seeking abortion, from whether a woman wants an abortion because she has been raped to whether she wants an abortion because it will impede her ability to qualify for her degree.

A doctor's judgement, in all these circumstances, rests on the extent to which he or she genuinely believes that an abortion will be less damaging to a woman's mental health than carrying the pregnancy to term. In this regard, a doctor who genuinely believes that a voluntary termination of an unwanted pregnancy will have no negative impact on a woman's mental health, but that having to give birth to a child will cause her some problems—for whatever reason—can make that good faith judgment.

Women Must Decide

The question is not, and cannot be, the content of the choice itself—a doctor cannot decide what the 'right' reason for an abortion is, not least because no such provision exists in our law. The only question is whether the woman feels that it is the best choice for her to make.

The tenor of Lansley's argument contradicts this subtle understanding of the British abortion law. He seems to recognise only that 'abortion is a life-changing decision', rather than understanding that abortion exists because bearing a child is a life-changing decision, and it is only through access to contraception and abortion that it is a decision at all, rather than simply a woman's fate.

Furthermore, his palpable distrust of doctors' role in negotiating the contours of the abortion law—summed up in his statement that for doctors 'simply' to 'flout' the abortion laws 'in a belief that they know better is unacceptable'—presumes that it should be doctors' role to prevent women from making bad (or, in the case of sex selection, 'morally repugnant') choices. According to this view, when health professionals 'support women in taking this decision', they should be checking that their decisions are good ones; and because doctors apparently cannot be trusted, 'it is why ... we are planning to consult on counselling arrangements for women seeking an abortion.'

These proposals are anathema to the spirit of non-directive counselling that has informed abortion care since the 1967 Act. Not only do they seek to make abortion decisions the preserve of healthcare professionals rather than the woman herself, but they seek to replace the clinical judgement of doctors with a gatekeeping role imposed by a new layer of more loosely-qualified counsellors, operating outside of the abortion service.

If the goal of this initiative is to make it more difficult for women to access abortions, it may well succeed. But it will be at the expense of clinical judgement, genuinely non-directive advice, and women's decision-making.

*"Sex-selective abortion has now come to
America ... and other countries ban
sex-selective abortion, but the U.S. ...
does not."*

Sex-Selective Abortion Must Be Banned in the United States to Prevent Gendercide of Girls

Keith Fournier

Keith Fournier is the editor in chief of Catholic Online, an informational website for Roman Catholics. In the following viewpoint he argues that sex-selective abortion and gendercide are becoming as serious a problem in the United States as they are abroad. He cites an undercover video investigation showing a Planned Parenthood worker trying to help a woman obtain an abortion on the grounds that the baby was a girl. Fournier contends that gendercide in the United States is aided by those who advocate for abortions. He argues that Congress should pass legislation making abortion for reasons of sex selection illegal.

As you read, consider the following questions:

1. According to Fournier, why is it not a surprise that sex-selective abortion occurs in the United States?

2. In what situations does the proposed bill against sex-selective abortion say that US law prohibits discrimination on the basis of sex, according to the author?

3. Which countries does Fournier say ban sex-selective abortion?

On Wednesday May 30, 2012, the United States House of Representatives will vote on the Prenatal Nondiscrimination Act (PRENDA) of 2012, House Bill 3541 [outlawing sex-selective abortion].

The fact that this horrendous practice takes place in the United States of America should come as no surprise. After all, abortion, the intentional taking of innocent human life in the womb, is legal in America, for any reason. However, many people do not know that includes the practice of gendercide, the intentional killing of a child because of his or her gender.

As a Nation we have rightly decried the intentional abortion of baby girls in India and China. We know that the practice of gendercide reveals and compounds the horrid reality of discrimination against women at every level of those societies. However, many Americans are unaware of the existence of such a practice in our own Nation. The introductory language of the Bill explains the injustice of the practice quite well:

Women are a vital part of American society and culture and possess the same fundamental human rights and civil rights as men. United States law prohibits the dissimilar treatment of males and females who are similarly situated and prohibits sex discrimination in various contexts, including the provision of employment, education, housing, health insurance coverage, and athletics.

Sex is an immutable characteristic ascertainable at the earliest stages of human development through existing medical technology and procedures commonly in use, including maternal-fetal bloodstream DNA sampling, amniocentesis, chorionic villus sampling or "CVS", and obstetric ultrasound. In addition to medically assisted sex determination, a growing sex determination niche industry has developed and is marketing low cost commercial products, widely advertised and available, that aid in the sex determination of an unborn child without the aid of medical professionals.

Experts have demonstrated that the sex-selection industry is on the rise and predict that it will continue to be a growing trend in the United States. Sex determination is always a necessary step to the procurement of a sex-selection abortion. A "sex-selection abortion" is an abortion undertaken for purposes of eliminating an unborn child based on the sex or gender of the child.

Sex selection abortion is barbaric, and described by scholars and civil rights advocates as an act of sex-based or gender-based violence, predicated on sex discrimination. Sex-selection abortions are typically late-term abortions performed in the 2nd or 3rd trimester of pregnancy, after the unborn child has developed sufficiently to feel pain.

Substantial medical evidence proves that an unborn child can experience pain at 20 weeks after conception, and perhaps substantially earlier. By definition, sex-selection abortions do not implicate the health of the mother of the unborn, but instead are elective procedures motivated by sex or gender bias.

Abortion on Demand

It would seem that such a barbaric procedure as gendercide would be decried unanimously by the members of the US House of Representatives, right? Sadly, the answer is no. This

Bill faces an uphill struggle. Abortion on demand is considered the "third rail"[1] in American politics by too many elected representatives.

In addition, the Bill is being opposed by strong, well funded interest groups who want to protect abortion of any kind, for diverse reasons. Some of these groups purport to protect women while they fail to oppose a practice which kills baby girls in the womb. You talk about a War on Women?[2] Now that's a real war on women, kill them before they are born and call it a "right". Pure Evil!

Some of the people who oppose this Bill publicly argue that the practice does not occur in the United States. They are absolutely wrong. Just how wrong was underscored on Tuesday, May 29, 2012, when Live Action, the heroic organization founded by Lila Rose, released an undercover video. . . .

Sex-Selective Abortion Exposed

The video is the first in a series entitled "Gendercide: Sex Selection in America". This stunning first installment is entitled "The War on Baby Girls". The interchange between the Planned Parenthood employee and the woman seeking a late term abortion because she is having a baby girl and wants a baby boy exposes not only the barbarism of Planned Parenthood but the existence of sex selection abortion in the United States of America. That is why the video is meeting such a fierce response from the opponents of the Fundamental Human Right to life and the Abortion Industry.

Here is an excerpt from the exchange offered by Live Action, followed by details for those who want to support their important work:

1. The "third rail" refers to the electrified rail that powers a subway train. People often commit suicide by jumping onto it and being electrocuted. So metaphorically, an issue referred to as the "third rail" means it is not something a politician wants to "touch" lest he or she commit career suicide.
2. The phrase "war on women" is sometimes used by Democrats to describe Republican policies seen as restricting women's rights.

Evidence of Sex Selection in the United States

Sex-selective abortion is also present in the United States. Researchers at the National Academy of Sciences (NAS) examined the 2000 U.S. Census and found that certain Asian-American families were significantly more likely than other Americans to have a boy if they already had a girl. "This male bias is particularly evident for third children," researchers found. "If there was no previous son, sons outnumbered daughters by 50 percent." A 2008 NAS report found similar results.

New technology could aggravate the problem. Pregnant women can now buy the Intelligender Gender Prediction Test for about $35 at their local chain pharmacy. The test boasts that it can discern the sex of a child with 82 percent accuracy, as early as ten weeks after conception and at home, with no need to visit a doctor's office.

Women who are really serious about giving birth to a child of the desired sex can undergo a procedure called pre-implantation genetic diagnosis [PGD]. PGD involves examining embryos resulting from in vitro fertilization, testing them for X or Y chromosomes, then implanting the desired embryos into a woman's womb.

A 2002 *Fortune* magazine survey found that 25 to 35 percent of parents and prospective parents said they would use sex selection if it were available.

Kate Obenshain, Divider-in-Chief: The Fraud of Hope and Change, *2012.*

"I see that you're saying that you want to terminate if it's a girl, so are you just wanting to continue the pregnancy in the meantime?" a counselor named "Rebecca" offers the woman, who is purportedly still in her first trimester and cannot be certain about the gender. "The abortion covers you up until 23 weeks," explains Rebecca, "and usually at 5 months is usually (sic) when they detect, you know, whether or not it's a boy or a girl." Doctors agree that the later in term a doctor performs an abortion, the greater the risk of complications.

The Planned Parenthood staffer suggests that the woman get on Medicaid in order to pay for an ultrasound to determine the gender of her baby, even though she plans to use the knowledge for an elective abortion. She also tells the woman to "just continue and try again" for the desired gender after aborting a girl, and adds, "Good luck, and I hope that you do get your boy."

"The search-and-destroy targeting of baby girls through prenatal testing and abortion is a pandemic that is spreading across the globe," notes Lila Rose, founder and president of Live Action. "Research proves that sex-selective abortion has now come to America. The abortion industry, led by Planned Parenthood, is a willing participant."

Six studies in the past four years indicate that there are thousands of "missing girls" in the U.S., many from sex-selective abortion. The U.K., India, Australia, and other countries ban sex-selective abortion, but the U.S., save for three states, does not. On Wednesday, Congress will debate the Prenatal Non-Discrimination Act (PRENDA), which would ban sex-selective abortions nationally.

"Planned Parenthood and their ruthless abortion-first mentality is the real 'war on women,'" says Rose. "Sex-selective abortion is gender discrimination with lethal consequences for little girls."

"Anyone who is genuinely concerned about sex-selective abortion should be working to fight sexism, its underlying cause. Laws that seek to limit women's autonomy and confine them to traditional roles have it precisely backward."

Banning Sex-Selective Abortion in the United States Will Only Increase Sexism and the Gendercide of Girls

Michelle Goldberg

Michelle Goldberg is a senior contributing writer for the news and commentary website Daily Beast *and the author of* The Means of Reproduction: Sex, Power, and the Future of the World. *In the following viewpoint, she argues that abortion for reasons of sex selection is not a serious problem in the United States. She adds that outlawing sex-selective abortion is not an effective response to gendercide. Rather, countries that have reduced sex-selective abortions, like South Korea, have done so by raising standards of living and the status of women. She suggests that if conservatives in the United States want to reduce sex-selective abortion, they should try to increase women's autonomy and power rather than putting restrictions on women's abortion rights.*

As you read, consider the following questions:

1. What is Live Action's modus operandi in its video series, according to Goldberg?

2. Why does the author question the figure of 100,000 women missing because of infanticide and abortion?

3. What does Goldberg say is the legal status of abortion in South Korea?

It's not surprising that anti-abortion activists see sex-selective abortion as their trump card. The issue puts feminists in a particularly difficult spot, turning reproductive choice into a tool of misogyny. Reporting on sex-selective abortion in India, where feminists campaign against *kanya bhronn hatya*—literally, "the killing of young girls"—and patriarchs angrily assert their right to plan their families, I sometimes felt like I'd stepped through a looking glass. Clearly, the American anti-abortion movement would be happy to frame the debate in similar terms.

Live Action vs. Planned Parenthood

That's exactly what activists now are trying to do. On Tuesday [May 29, 2012], the day before the House debated a bill to ban sex-selective abortions, the anti-abortion group Live Action released a video titled "Gendercide: Sex Selection in America," shot undercover at a Planned Parenthood clinic in Austin [Texas]. (It is apparently Part 1 in a series.) The idea is to paint abortion clinics as aggressors in the war on women and thus limit abortion rights on ostensibly feminist grounds.

Live Action's MO [modus operandi, or way of working] is to send operatives into Planned Parenthood clinics with hid-

den cameras and stories meant to put staffers in morally com-
promising positions. In this case, the activist poses as a pregnant woman who wants to abort if she's carrying a girl. Her
interaction with a Planned Parenthood employee named
Rebecca is disturbing, particularly as edited in the *Gendercide*
video. Planned Parenthood, rightly, does not turn women
away because it objects to their reasons for seeking abortion,
but Rebecca still seems rather too encouraging, ending their
encounter with a chipper, "Good luck, and I hope you do get
your boy!" (Rebecca was fired shortly after the video was shot
in April.)

None of this, though, proves that Planned Parenthood is
complicit in "gendercide."

To its credit, Live Action also has posted a seemingly
unedited version of the video on its website protectour-
girls.com, which complicates the picture a little bit, even if it
doesn't change the central dynamic. In the longer video, the
operative says she and her husband want two children, a boy
and a girl, and that they already have a girl. Because the issue
is family balance rather than misogyny, there would be no
point in Rebecca trying to convince her of the value of daughters. Similarly, in the longer video, Rebecca clearly tells the
woman that Planned Parenthood doesn't do sex determination ultrasounds but that she shouldn't have trouble finding a
place that does.

The operative repeatedly expresses her fear of being judged
and at one point even asks how she can rationalize her decision to disapproving friends. Rather than offering a defense of
sex selection, Rebecca gives her a list of counselors who, she
says, "might give you better choices, and words, in terms of
your decision." Rebecca probably should have pushed counseling more insistently and found a way to show understanding
without approval. But it is not the job of anyone at Planned
Parenthood to talk women out of their choices, even if those
choices seem callous.

Sex Ratios in the United States, 2013

Age range	Male to female ratio
At birth	1.05
0–14 years	1.04
15–24 years	1.04
25–54 years	1
55–64 years	0.93
65 years and older	0.77
Total population	0.97

TAKEN FROM: CIA, "Field Listing: Sex Ratio," *The World Fact Book*, 2013. www.cia.gov.

Nevertheless, Live Action's video will likely be a potent weapon in the ongoing effort to discredit Planned Parenthood and undermine abortion rights. It can't be a coincidence that the video came out just as the House took up the Prenatal Non-Discrimination Act, which would imprison doctors who perform sex-selective abortions and force them to report women they suspect of seeking such terminations. That act would represent a major change in federal law, which does not currently give the government a say in whether a woman's reasons for having an abortion are valid.

In the end, the Prenatal Non-Discrimination Act will probably fail [it did]. It's being brought to a vote under a suspension of House rules, which means it needs a two-thirds majority to pass. It's a maneuver that allows Republicans to raise the issue without being held accountable for trying to change the law. Things are different at the state level, though; Illinois, Oklahoma, Arizona, and Pennsylvania already prohibit sex-selective abortion, and other states are likely to join them.

Prohibiting Sex-Selective Abortion

One might fairly ask, of course, what's wrong with that. Worldwide, after all, sex-selective abortion is a serious problem. Live Action's video begins by proclaiming that, globally, 100,000,000 women are missing because of infanticide and abortion. This is a distortion, but the reality is still troubling.

Live Action's figure comes from work by Nobel Prize–winning economist Amartya Sen, who estimates that the world has 100,000,000 fewer women than it should because of a whole host of disparities in "health, medicine, and nutrition." Female infanticide and sex-selective abortion are part of a much larger problem. Still, there's no question that sex-selective abortion is leading to a crisis in much of Asia, creating societies with lopsided gender ratios that in turn lead to greater sexual violence and the potential for serious instability. I've been to districts in northern India with fewer than 800 girls for every 1,000 boys. Not only does this signal a terrifying devaluation of women, it exacerbates the issue.

Crude economic logic might suggest that a shortage of women would raise their social worth. In fact, it tends to increase sex trafficking and to push women to marry younger. Meanwhile, a surplus of unmarriageable young men can be seriously destabilizing. As the political scientists Valerie M. Hudson and Andrea M. den Boer write in their book *Bare Branches: The Security Implications of Asia's Surplus Male Population*, societies where men outnumber women "breed chronic violence and persistent social disorder and corruption."

Sex Selection and the United States

None of this, however, applies to the United States. There is some evidence of sex selection among Asian immigrants in this country, though it's unclear whether that is happening through abortion or IVF [in vitro fertilization]. Overall, though, our sex ratios are normal. An extremely rare phenomenon is thus being used in an effort to set a far-reaching precedent. Sex-selective abortion is odious. Banning it means allowing the government to decide what constitutes a legitimate reason for a woman to terminate a pregnancy, and forcing doctors to try to discern the motives of their patients.

South Korea is the one country in the world where there's been genuine progress in reducing the incidence of sex-selective abortion. It didn't happen through an abortion ban—abortion in that country has long been illegal, though widely available. What changed is that women's status improved and archaic traditions started to lose their power. In most Asian countries, there's a temporary correlation between increased wealth and education and sex selection, because privileged people have the most access to the relevant technology. But as South Korea shows, eventually, social change catches up.

"Avenues opened up for obtaining livelihoods and social status which were independent of lineage membership and adherence to familial expectations," wrote Woojin Chung and Monica Das Gupta in a 2007 paper for the World Bank that sought to explain why sex ratios in South Korea were improving. "The accompanying urbanization resulted in people no longer being surrounded by patrilineal kin in their place of residence and work. This also opened up a possibility for relationships between parents and their children to be driven by affect rather than by rigid rules of gender and birth order. All these changes helped undercut the bases for son preference."

The lesson is clear. Anyone who is genuinely concerned about sex-selective abortion should be working to fight sexism, its underlying cause. Laws that seek to limit women's autonomy and confine them to traditional roles have it precisely backward. Unless, of course, limiting women's autonomy and confining them to traditional roles has been the goal all along.

> *"In Canada, doctors rarely perform abortions after 22 weeks of pregnancy unless the baby has a lethal fetal abnormality or the mother's life is in danger due to the pregnancy."*

Selective Abortions Prompt Call For Later Ultrasounds

Huffington Post

The Huffington Post *is an online newspaper and blog covering a wide range of topics, including breaking news, politics, and entertainment. The following viewpoint examines the argument of Rajendar Kale, editor-in-chief of the* Canadian Medical Journal, *who feels that the gender of a fetus should not be given out until after 30 weeks of pregnancy. Kale believes that the gender of a fetus should be withheld until this time to prevent abortions of female fetuses, which Kale argues is a common occurence among certain groups. The Society of Obstetricians and Gynecologists of Canada disagrees with Kale, arguing that it is a patient's right to know the gender of her fetus.*

As you read, consider the following questions:

1. What does Kale say is the starting point of female feticide from a health-care perspective?

2. Does the Society of Obstetricians and Gynecologists of Canada agree with Kale, that the gender of a fetus should be withheld until after 30 weeks of pregnancy?

3. What evidence does Kale provide that sex-selective abortion is occurring in Canada?

A fetus's gender should not be revealed until after 30 weeks of pregnancy, says an editorial published in the *Canadian Medical Journal*.

This change in procedure for a fetal ultrasound—where the sex is usually disclosed to parents at 20 weeks—would help prevent female feticide, says Rajendar Kale, editor in chief of the CMAJ.

In Canada, doctors rarely perform abortions after 22 weeks of pregnancy unless the baby has a lethal fetal abnormality or the mother's life is in danger due to the pregnancy.

Kale says that in countries such as India, China, Korea and Vietnam, female fetuses are commonly aborted because of a preference for sons. Though by no means widespread, the practice is carried out by some immigrants to Canada, Kale says.

His editorial cites a small U.S. study that found 40 per cent of 65 immigrant Indian women surveyed had terminated earlier pregnancies and 89 per cent terminated their current pregnancies when they discovered they were having girls. Previous Canadian research has suggested that sex selection is occurring in Canada in certain groups when families have had girls and are seeking a son. The practice has created a gender imbalance in these communities.

"A pregnant woman being told the sex of the fetus at ultrasonography at a time when an unquestioned abortion is possible is the starting point of female feticide from a healthcare perspective," writes Kale. "The solution is to postpone the disclosure of medically irrelevant information to women until after about 30 weeks of pregnancy."

Abortion in Canada

On 28 January 1988. the Supreme Court of Canada in *R. v. Morgentaler* struck down the country's abortion law as contrary to the *Charter of Rights and Freedoms*. The court ruled that the law violated a woman's security of person not only by forcing her to carry a foetus to term under threat of criminal sanction, but also by causing lengthy delays in obtaining an abortion, thereby increasing her risk of physical and psychological harm. The Crown had argued that women who had difficulty procuring a legal abortion in their home communities could travel to access pregnancy termination elsewhere. Yet in rendering the decision of the majority, Chief Justice Brian Dickson countered that the law . . . burdened women unduly. He recognized that as a result of the law, many women were forced to travel, often at enormous emotional and financial expense, to seek abortion services in other jurisdictions.

In the 20 years since the Morgentaler decision, there has been no federal law regulating abortion in Canada. Now abortion is purportedly fully funded under the *Canada Health Act* as a "medically necessary" service. Abortion services are available domestically in public sector hospitals as well as in private and public sector for-profit and non-profit clinics.

Christabelle Setha and Marion Doull, in Critical Interventions in the Ethics of Health Care: Challenging the Principle of Autonomy in Bioethics, *2009.*

Kale wants to see gender disclosure policies at 30 weeks adopted by the provincial colleges that govern doctors. "Such clear direction from regulatory bodies would be the most important step toward curbing female feticide in Canada."

The Society of Obstetricians and Gynecologists of Canada said Kale's proposal is inconsistent with their policy, which states that "a patient's request for disclosure should be respected, either directly or in a report to the referring health professional."

In an email to CBC News, the obstetricians group said it believes it is the right of the patient to be informed of the gender of the fetus, and that this information should not be withheld.

The editorial also did not consider tests on the market that give expectant parents a fetal sex determination of high accuracy as early as eight weeks into a pregnancy, the group noted.

"The SOGC in no way condones pregnancy termination based on non-medical reasons, such as the gender of the fetus. The SOGC feels strongly that it is the cultural values and norms in specific segments of the Canadian population that must change to ensure that females are not confronted with procedures and intolerant environments before or after they are born."

| *"If we refuse ... ultrasound information in 'non-ethnic' areas of Toronto to fore-stall 'bad abortions' in others, this is racism piled on racism."*

Restricting Ultrasound Information in Canada Is Morally Wrong and Will Not Prevent Gendercide

Heather Mallick

Heather Mallick is an author and a columnist for the Toronto Star, *a daily newspaper. In the following viewpoint, she argues that the evidence that Asian women in Canada are aborting girls is not definitive. She also says that women's abortion decisions should not be questioned, and that the push to deny Asian women ultrasound information is sexist and racist. She concludes that the best way to reduce sex-selective abortion is to improve the status of women and end sexism in Canada.*

As you read, consider the following questions:

    1. What evidence indicates that some families in Canada may be sex selecting for girls, according to Mallick?

Heather Mallick, "Hiding Toronto Hospital Ultrasound Results to Prevent Sex Selection Is Pointless—And Possibly Racist," *Toronto Star*, April 17, 2012.

2. What does the author state that Canadian law says about abortion?

3. What evidence does Mallick provide that social norms change with time?

The need to control women and their bodies is a never-ending quest.

Many GTA [greater Toronto area] hospitals, particularly those in "ethnic" areas, the *Star* reported Tuesday [April 17, 2012], won't let their ultrasound staff tell pregnant women the sex of the fetus. One admitted it worries that women and their spouses (if any) might have the female fetus aborted in order to try again for a male.

A recent study done by St. Michael's Hospital researchers has shown that though the male/female ratio for the first child of immigrants born in India is normal Canadian stuff—105 boys to 100 girls—the ratio for third children born to such women was 136 boys to 100 girls. This may mean something. This may mean something wildly other than what it seems.

The study, inspired by a *Canadian Medical Association Journal* editorial calling sex-selection "repugnant," has many limitations, its three authors admit. Ethnicity, personal family history and multi-fetal pregnancies, all these areas remain blurry. These are overall figures, with hypotheses.

As if it matters in the end. Ultrasounds are here to stay. Refusing to say "girl" or "boy" is akin to those languid doctor committees of yore that decided whether a desperate woman would be allowed her abortion or not. Canadian women have control over their own bodies. Is this to be denied to Canadians of South Asian and South Korean origin?

It's not our business.

The *Star* recently quoted Toronto "bioethicist" Tom Koch on pregnant women who choose to abort a fetus with Down syndrome. "We're engaged in eugenics [breeding out unwanted traits], sure," he said, going on to blithely deplore heartbroken couples who realize they can't cope with a disabled child or a second disabled child.

"Eugenics" has a horrific ring to it, just as the medical term "feticide" sounds worse than "abortion" and is used by this study's authors.

A Personal Decision

But Canadian law says abortion is a personal decision. I'm mystified by those who say it's ironic that feminists wanted choice and now that choice is reducing the number of females born. Women aren't Toyota, looking to increase market share. We're individuals.

Go blame ultrasounds, not women, the same ultrasounds that primitive southern U.S. states force women to undergo to shame them pre-abortion. Ultrasounds, so handy in Texas, so fraught in Brampton. The sexism in this medical story simply reeks.

So there are "good" abortions and "bad" abortions, good parents and "bad" aborters. If these sex-selective abortions are common among Canadian immigrants born in India and South Korea and sex-selection is bad, does that mean that white women are by definition good? Because they have their preferences, too, maybe for a balanced family.

Some women just want a healthy baby. Some women only want girls. Who knows, maybe they dread having to play endless games of catch in the backyard. My Italian girlfriend was elated when she gave birth to two boys. Thank god they weren't girls, she whispered to me. My daughters' lives would have been so hard.

I don't leap to judgment of any woman seeking an abortion. No one should. By deploring sex-selection—if that's what this is and we don't yet know that—we're saying "this is a bad reason to have an abortion." But if we refuse the same ultrasound information in "non-ethnic" areas of Toronto to forestall "bad abortions" in others, this is racism piled on racism.

Social norms do change with time. The *Economist* reports that between 1985 and 2003, the share of South Korean women who said they felt "they must have a son" fell by almost two-thirds, from 48 per cent to 17 per cent. Industrialization and prosperity change female prospects. There is hope.

Here's an idea. Why don't we show immigrants from South Asia how fair-minded Canada is toward women? As well you know, 87.2 per cent of the House of Commons is female, there is no wage gap and when women go for their ultrasound, the results aren't snatched away from them with a "That's for me to know and you to find out, young lady."

When immigrants see how women are treated, they'll realize that girls and boys have an equal chance in Canadian life. Problem solved. You're welcome.

Periodical and Internet Sources Bibliography

The following articles have been selected to supplement the diverse views presented in this chapter.

Ross Douthat	"When Is Sex-Selective Abortion a 'Problem?,'" *New York*, May 31, 2012.
Cameron English	"Sex Selection of Fetuses Is a Parental Right," *PolicyMic*, October 2012. www.policymic.com.
Steven Ertelt	"Report Shows Illegal Sex-Selection Abortions Happening in UK," LifeNews.com, January 11, 2013. www.lifenews.com.
Nancy French	"Sex Selective Abortion: A Plea to Fathers," *National Review*, July 12, 2012.
General Medical Council	"Sex Selection and Abortion: Keep Within the Law," August 22, 2012. www.gmc-uk.org.
Sujatha Jesudason and Anat Shenker-Osorio	"Sex Selection in America: Why It Persists and How We Can Change It," *Atlantic Monthly*, May 31, 2012.
Barbara Kay	"Barbara Kay on Sex-Selective Abortion: The Real 'War on Women' That Dares Not Speak Its Name," *National Post*, December 19, 2012.
Amanda Marcotte	"Anti-choice Bill Just Part of a Growing List of Anti-woman Legislation." *XX Factor* (blog), *Slate*, May 31, 2012. www.slate.com.
Rowena Mason	"The Abortion of Unwanted Girls Taking Place in the UK," *Daily Telegraph* (London), January 10, 2013.
Laura Payton	"MP's Motion on Sex Selection Stirs Abortion Debate," CBC News, December 5, 2012. www.cbc.ca.

CHAPTER 3

What Is the Relationship Between Gender-Related Violence and Genocide?

Chapter Preface

In 1971, Bangladesh declared independence from Pakistan, setting off a civil war and one of the worst genocides of the twentieth century. The genocide was strongly influenced by gender. Boys and young men were especially targeted as potential fighters or resisters. According to R.J. Rummell, quoted by Adam Jones on the Gendercide Watch website, "Sweeps were conducted of young men who were never seen again. Bodies of youths would be found in fields, floating down rivers, or near army camps." Young men in fear of their lives would flee from village to village, trying to get to India and safety. The targeting of elites in universities and intellectual occupations also effectively meant the targeting of men, since few women occupied these positions.

Alongside the male gendercide occurred a brutal systematic program of rape directed against women. Between two hundred thousand and four hundred thousand Bangladeshi women were raped during the conflict. Rape was used as a deliberate act of terror to subjugate the Bangladeshi population. Many of the victims were girls as young as thirteen.

After the conflict, the leader of Bangladesh, Sheikh Mujibur Rahman, tried to help the victims return to their communities by calling them "war heroines." But according to Anushay Hossain, writing in a May 21, 2012, article in the US financial magazine *Forbes*, "The gesture largely did not work. After being assaulted and impregnated by Pakistani soldiers, the Bangladeshi women were completely ostracized by society. Many were killed by their husbands, committed suicide, or murdered their half-Pakistani babies themselves."

An International Criminal Tribunal in Bangladesh has begun to try to issue indictments forty years after the ending of the conflict. But Irene Khan, former secretary general of Amnesty International, is not convinced that those who orchestrated the mass rapes will be found or brought to justice. In an August 24, 2010, article by Nilanjana S. Roy in the *New York Times*, Khan pointed out that "Bangladesh remains a conservative, patriarchic society where women's role continues to be undervalued—past or present."

The viewpoints in this chapter will examine other instances in which gendercide and gender-related violence has been a part of genocide.

| *"Gendercide" is as legitimate a phrase as 'genocide.'"*

Gendercide Is Closely Related to Genocide

Heather McRobie

At this writing, Heather McRobie was a PhD student, the author of the novel Psalm 119, *and a writer for the* Guardian, New Statesmen, *and other British publications. In the following viewpoint, she argues that gendercide, or the targeted killing of individuals because of their gender, is an important term. She says that it helps makes sense of killings of men in the Serbian conflict, and of women in places like Guatemala and Ciudad Juárez, Mexico. She concludes that because of its parallel with the term genocide, or racial killing, the term gendercide can help establish the importance of gendered violence and so help to understand and prevent it.*

As you read, consider the following questions:

1. Why does McRobie say that the Bosnian killings were a gendercide?

2. If the term *gendercide* is not used, how does McRobie fear killings in Guatemala will be dismissed?

3. How does cultural relativism excuse acts of gendered violence, according to the author?

Changing our terminology won't stop mass killings, I know that. But it might go some way toward more fully comprehending—and better campaigning against—some of the worst atrocities of our time. Just as "genocide" refers to a systematic killing of a race or ethnicity, so "gendercide" refers to the systematic killing of a gender. Although Amnesty International and other groups have been right to push for the term "femicide" to describe the murder of hundreds of women in Ciudad Juárez in Mexico and Guatemala City, on the whole it'd be more helpful to use the more neutral term "gendercide" to help raise awareness of the issue, as, evidently, the victims are not always women.

Targeted by Gender

One such case is Srebrenica, the subject of renewed analysis—although it shouldn't take a news story to remind us of it—after the capture of [Serbian leader Radovan] Karadzic last week [July 2008]. It is widely acknowledged that the killing of 8,000 Bosnian men and boys was part of a policy to kill as many non-combatant males as possible, in order to reduce the pool of possible enemy soldiers. Recognising that this was a gendercide is completely compatible with recognising that it was a genocide, a fact which has been long established. The victims of Srebrenica and similar massacres ordered by Karadzic were targeted because of their ethnicity. But they were also targeted because of their gender.

To refer to Srebrenica as a gendercide doesn't imply that one gender's suffering in a war was somehow more important than the other's. Linda Grant's piece on rape as a weapon of war in Bosnia is a reminder of how women were brutally targeted throughout the conflict. But when a rape occurs during peace-time, we tend to think of it as a violent, misogynistic act. When a rape occurs during war time, we tend to think of it as a violent, racist act—an atrocity motivated by the ethnicity of the victim. We need to start recognising that war is gendered in reality, that in this arena women are not raped solely for being women or solely for their ethnicity, but for the combination of the two. For me, feminism has always been about how rigid gender roles harm everyone, albeit primarily women. And during a war, rigid gender roles, like rigid ethnic stereotypes, lead to a differentiated targeting of civilians.

One counter-argument I anticipate in reply to this is that, as "gendercide" is a less potent phrase than "genocide" (in part by virtue of it still being largely unknown), using it may seem to belittle the genocide committed in Bosnia. But no one is arguing that gender is the main reason for the mass murders in most cases—although it does seem to be the primary element in the gendercides of Ciudad Juárez and Guatemala City. It was, however, an element of the mass killings in Bosnia, and we ignore it at our peril. As a whole, we have little framework for the concept of intersecting discriminations, and until we can formulate a succinct way of expressing the multi-dimensional nature of oppression, to refer to Srebrenica as a genocide and a gendercide may be the best way we can convey the various aspects that were at work.

Not Random Acts

Rather than belittling mass killings, moreover, using the phrase "gendercide" in other contexts has the opposite effect: it becomes an important way to convey the true scale and nature of gender-based murders, which are otherwise often dismissed as a conglomerate of discrete phenomena, the product of a few bad eggs. Until we routinely conceptualise the murders of women in Guatemala City and Ciudad Juárez as gendercides—as killings directed specifically against one section of a

Femicide in Guatemala

Today [2010] women in Guatemala are killed at nearly the same rate as they were in the early 1980s when the civil war became genocidal. Yet the current femicide epidemic is less an aberration than a reflection of the way violence against women has become normalized in Guatemala. Used to re-inscribe patriarchy and sustain both dictatorships and democracies, gender-based violence morphed into femicide when peacetime governments became too weak to control extralegal and paramilitary powers. The naturalization of gender-based violence over the course of the twentieth century maintained and promoted the systemic impunity that undergirds femicide today. . . .

Since 2000, more than five thousand women and girls have been brutally murdered in Guatemala. Their bodies litter city streets, urban ravines, and the imagination of the media. Images of murdered women and girls are so commonplace that each new death risks becoming a footnote to illustrate a rising death toll. These femicides take place in a country that has become infamous for having one of the region's top homicide rates. In 2007, for example, Guatemalans were killed at a rate of 41.8 people per 100,000, compared to U.S. figures of 5.6 people per 100,000 in the same year.

David Carey Jr. and M. Gabriela Torres,
Latin American Research Review, *2010.*

population—the tragedies will continue to be dismissed as essentially random acts. It's hard to account for the shocking police impunity to the murders in Juárez, but it seems that the Mexican police's position is, essentially, that a few men happen to kill some women, and that's all very sad, but not something society as a whole should feel responsible for, or be concerned about.

The evocation of the word "genocide" in the word "gendercide"—the implication, that, like genocide, it is a crime against humanity for which there are no excuses—would also counter the dead-end cultural relativism that feminists have to deal with from across the spectrum whenever they speak out against gender-based violence. One of the things that is so frustrating about cultural relativism is not its central philosophical tenet so much as the fact it is used so inconsistently by its proponents—no one (I hope) ever says of apartheid South Africa: "Well, that was just their culture, who are we to judge?" The systematic oppression of a whole race is not a legitimate part of anyone's culture. But the systematic oppression of a gender? Whenever I raise the topic of countries whose treatment of women could largely be termed a "gender apartheid", the response in liberal circles is: "well, that's their culture, let's not be imperialist". As though apartheid was a temporal, historical act, within the reach of our moral judgment, whereas "culture" must be treated as an innate, ahistorical phenomenon which renders it impossible to judge. Why do gender roles get pushed into the play-pen of "culture", beyond time and beyond criticism, when ethnicity, it is accepted, is a constructed identity that changes over time, defined and redefined, and manipulated by ultra-nationalists like Karadzic? Is the murder of female children in India and China more forgivable, on the grounds of "culture", than the mass murder of ethnic groups?

A Legitimate Phrase

Surely unless you're prepared to stand up and admit: yes, I think it is worse to discriminate on the grounds of race than on gender, then "gendercide" is as legitimate a phrase as "genocide", and we should be as ready to speak out against it as we are against racial- or ethnicity-based violence. As Karadzic is finally brought to justice, I hope we take into account all the dimensions of the mass killings he and [Serb military leader Ratko] Mladic ordered, so that we can finally begin to make sense of what happened in Bosnia, and prevent it from happening again.

> *"Genocide is the mass killing of a group of humans. It does not matter what group of humans!"*

Gendercide Is Genocide

Rita Banerji

Rita Banerji is the founder of the 50 Million Missing campaign to end ongoing female genocide in India. In the following viewpoint she argues that gendercide fits the technical definition of genocide, since genocide is the targeted killing of a specific group of humans, and women constitute a specific human group. She says that the killing of women was left out of the UN definition of genocide because of sexism and a lack of attention to the plight of women. She concludes that the use of the label genocide is vital to organizing human rights resistance to the violence against women in India.

As you read, consider the following questions:

1. How does the UN article Banerji cites define genocide?

2. How does Peter Drost define genocide, as quoted by the author?

Rita Banerji, "Why Is the Annihilation of India's Women Genocide?," *The 50 Million Missing Campaign (blog)*, June 26, 2011. www.50millionmissing.info. Copyright © 2011 by Rita Benerji. All rights reserved. Reproduced by permission.

3. How does Banerji suggest that *femicide* differs from the term *genocide*?

Someone left a message on my flickr site, on my posting on the female genocide in India. He said, *"The word 'genocide' doesn't apply here; it only cheapens the word."*

I asked him to explain. He said, *"This situation does not fit the legal definition of genocide [as in] the 1948 United Nations Convention on the Prevention and Punishment of the Crime of Genocide (CPPCG)."*

The U.N. Article defines genocide as:

(a) Killing members of the group;

(b) Causing serious bodily or mental harm to members of the group;

(c) Deliberately inflicting on the group conditions of life calculated to bring about its physical destruction in whole or in part;

(d) Imposing measures intended to prevent births within the group.

I counter argued. *"Actually this is a genocide based on that very legal definition of genocide."* Females are being killed in India at every stage of life, before and after birth, *only because they are female.* This is not happening to boys and men! This is a MASS and TARGETED elimination of *a specific group.*

More than 50 million women have been killed in India in 3 generations. More than a million female fetuses are selectively aborted every year. Medical companies in the West are racing to provide newer technologies to this female-hating market. Thousands of newborn girls are strangled, drowned or buried. Girls under 5 years of age have a 75% higher mortality rate than boys that age, due to deliberate starvation and neglect and also due to various forms of inflicted violence. More than 100,000 young women are gang-lynched by their

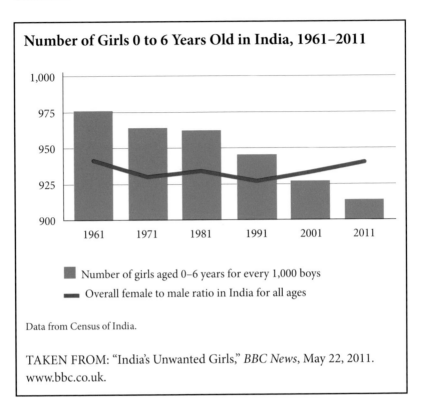

Number of Girls 0 to 6 Years Old in India, 1961–2011

- Number of girls aged 0–6 years for every 1,000 boys
- Overall female to male ratio in India for all ages

Data from Census of India.

TAKEN FROM: "India's Unwanted Girls," *BBC News*, May 22, 2011. www.bbc.co.uk.

husbands and in-laws in dowry related murders every year. Thousands more, who don't succumb to the attempts to burn, hang or poison them, live with physical and emotional trauma. Every 5 minutes, 1 pregnant woman dies, often because women are forced by their husbands and in-laws to undergo repeated abortions to rid potential daughters.

Female genocide in India is the result of an extremely virulent misogyny just as the Jewish genocide was the result of an extremely virulent anti-Semitism. Then why should this dehumanization and mass extermination of women not be recognized as a 'genocide'?

My flickr visitor had a very simple answer. He said because the U.N. definition applies only to the case of "a national, ethnical, racial or religious group." But in the legal definition there is no mention of gender!

I pointed out to him the obvious. This law was written in 1948. The men (certainly there were no women in that group) who sat around a table in 1948 and wrote up the U.N. Genocide article, were thinking in a time zone when women were not even considered a social human group. Countries in Europe, like Switzerland, at that time, did not even give women voting rights. The U.S., which had a history of black slavery, gave the right to vote to black men before women in general got the right to vote.

However, about a decade later, in 1959, Peter Drost (The Crime of State, Volume 2, Leiden, 1959, p. 125) said, "Genocide is the deliberate destruction of physical life of individual human beings by reason of their membership of any human collectivity as such."

And in 1994, Israel Charny affirmed, "Genocide in the generic sense means the mass killing of substantial numbers of human beings, under conditions of the essential defencelessness of the victim."

So I told my flickr visitor, "Genocide is the mass killing of a group of humans. It does not matter what group of humans!" And just to state the obvious—women are a human group!

Sometimes a conversation like this gets surreal. Here I am an Indian woman, arguing that the elimination of millions of Indian women (women like me) should be recognized as genocide when this man offered a sage piece of advice, "*Your cause is good and the situation of killing or aborting girls on the basis of gender is horrible. I am just saying that you are tending towards hyperbole and inaccurate terminology, and that is off-putting to people who want to deal with this disturbing problem in a precise and serious manner.*"

Not Just Gendercide

He further recommended that we just use the word "*Gendercide [because] it specifies the nature of the problem better than 'genocide', and it doesn't diminish the problem one bit.*"

Why this resistance to calling the mass extermination of women a genocide? We did not think that the mass extermination of Jews was Semiticide or that of Tutsis [in Rwanda] was Tutsicide. Regicide does not have to mean the mass and targetted killing of kings. It can even be the killing of one king. The same for matricide, patricide, infanticide. Gendercide is the killing of a person because they belong to a specific gender.

Femicide is the term that Diana Russell first used in 1976 to refer to misogynist killings; the killing of a person only because they are female. Female infanticide, honor killings, sati, dowry murders, witch huntings, are all examples of femicides in India. Even a single incident of female infanticide or dowry murder is a femicide. But what term do you use when MILLIONS who belong to a group are eliminated ONLY becaue they belong to that group?

A Necessary Strategy

Indeed, women form one of the two largest human groups! In fact, genetically, physiologically, biologically, and culturally, men and women as separate identifiable groups, are far more distinctly defined than human groups based on any other category such race, religion or ethnicity.

The recognition of the mass and targeted elimination of millions of women from India as 'female genocide' is a necessary strategy to drum up the kind of international human rights accountability and action required, across the board, from governments, to courts, to police and medical establishments—all agencies that are complicit in India's female genocide.

| "Serb forces used the rape of Muslims in
Bosnia as a tool of genocide."

Mass Rape of Women Can Be a Form of Genocide

Anthony Marino

Anthony Marino is a lawyer and at the time of writing the following viewpoint was a student at the Boston University School of Law. In the following viewpoint, he argues that rape was used as a weapon of genocide during the Bosnian war in the 1990s. He says that evidence indicates that Serbs deliberately raped and impregnated Bosnian Muslims in order to force them to bear Serbian children, which was an attempt to destroy Muslims as a group. Marino argues that the pattern of intentional, genocidal rape by Serbs was glossed over by the International Criminal Court because the court was reluctant to find Serbia guilty of intentional genocide.

As you read, consider the following questions:

1. Why did some feminists argue that Serb rapes should be seen as genocidal, while others argued they should not, in Marino's opinion?

2. For Serbs and Muslims, whose ethnicity determines the ethnicity of a child, according to the author?

3. In what ways is ethnic cleansing not necessarily the same as genocide, in Marino's view?

The women and children were separated into four groups at the police station and taken to separate houses confiscated from Muslim owners. The witness was placed with a group of 28 women. One of the soldiers told her that women, children, and old people were being taken to these homes because they were "not worth a bullet." They were kept in this house for 27 days.

Day and night, soldiers came to the house taking two to three women at a time. There were four to five guards at all times, all local Foca Serbs. The women knew the rapes would begin when "Mars Na Drinu" was played over the loudspeaker of the main mosque. ("Mars Na Drinu," or "March on the Drina," is reportedly a former "Chetnik" fighting song that was banned during the Tito years.)[1]

While "Mars Na Drinu" was playing, the women were ordered to strip and soldiers entered the homes, taking away the ones they wanted. The ages of women taken ranged from 12 to 60. Frequently the soldiers would seek out mother and daughter combinations. Many of the women were severely beaten during the rapes.

The witness was selected twice. The first time, soldiers had entered and grabbed an 18-year-old girl, asking her if she were a virgin. She said she was. Licking his knife, one of the soldiers said that if they found she was not, he would butcher her. The witness pleaded with them not [to] take the girl but to take her instead. "We'll take you, too," they said.

---

1. Marshal Josip Broz Tito was leader of Yugoslavia during the Cold War, from around 1945 to 1980. Serbia, Bosnia, and other Balkan nations had been lumped together during this time as "Yugoslavia."

While the witness was being raped, her rapist told her, "You should have already left this town. We'll make you have Serbian babies who will be Christians." Two soldiers raped her at that time; five soldiers raped the 18-year-old girl in full view of the witness.

Rape in War vs. Rape as Genocide

On March 20, 1993, Bosnia and Herzegovina (Bosnia) filed suit in the International Court of Justice (ICJ) against what was then the Federal Republic of Yugoslavia (FRY), alleging the latter's participation in a campaign of genocide against the non-Serb population of Bosnia and Herzegovina and seeking provisional measures to halt the continued atrocities ("the Genocide Case"). On April 8, 1993, the Court handed down provisional measures ordering the FRY to "ensure that any military, paramilitary or irregular armed units which may be directed or supported by it, as well as any organizations and persons which may be subject to its control, direction or influence" not commit, conspire to commit, incite, or be complicit in genocide. It would take almost fourteen more years for the court to rule on whether the atrocities committed against non-Serbs in Bosnia amounted to genocide, and if so, whether such acts or complicity in them could be attributed to the FRY and its successor. Among the issues the Court had to decide was whether systematic rape and sexual violence, as alleged by Bosnia, was carried out as a part of the genocidal campaign.

As Alexandra Stiglmayer pointed out in her piece, *The Rapes in Bosnia-Herzegovina*, "[w]omen have always been raped in wartime, of course. There were mass rapes even in wars that were not wars of expulsion. Rapes seem to be part and parcel of a soldier's life, a 'normal' accompaniment to war." But Stiglmayer tacitly acknowledges that there was something different about the rapes carried out by Serbian forces in Bosnia-Herzegovina, because, as she put it, "dispersion [was] precisely the goal."

The widespread and systematic rape of women in Bosnia-Herzegovina led to a divide in feminist scholarship on whether rape by one side in the conflict could, or should, be classified as "genocidal," thereby signaling a matter of heightened international concern. Karen Engle summarizes the competing views in this debate:

> If women were raped on all sides of the war and the feminist goal was to stop all rapes, then how could one choose sides in the conflict? Some feminists did choose sides, seeing the rapes by Serbian men as genocidal and therefore calling for extraordinary attention. Others disagreed, arguing that such a position would deny the extent to which women were always harmed in war, and were specifically harmed on all sides of the Balkan conflict. The latter position did not deny that rapes were hideous; far from it, those who expressed this view often argued that rapes on all sides might be considered "genocidal," but because of their effect on women as a group, not on Bosnian Muslim women in particular.

The outcome of the *Genocide Case* then could have had profound implications for this debate and might have helped to clarify when and how a campaign of rape and sexual violence targeted at a specific population would constitute genocide. Unfortunately, the Court did not address the issue of rape and sexual violence in any systematic way, and in the end, left the legal status of "rape as genocide" arguments more convoluted than before. In doing so, the Court disregarded or denied the existence of readily available evidence (in many cases, evidence from sources on which the Court relied heavily elsewhere in its decision) and rested on a questionable reading of the Convention, confounding specific intent with an act's success in achieving that intent. The purpose of this Note [an article in a law review] is to raise questions concerning the court's treatment of Bosnia's allegations that Serbia committed acts of genocide through rape and other sexual and reproductive violence, and to evaluate how its decision impacts the status of such violence as violations of international law relating to genocide. . . .

Forced Impregnation

The strongest support for Bosnia's assertions that Serbian rapists intended to prevent births within the Bosnian Muslim group came from the evidence of forced impregnation by Serbians whose goal was to make their victims have "Serb" babies. To consider a child resulting from a rape "Serb," the rapist would have to completely disregard the identity of the mother and believe that only his own ethnicity would pass on to the child. Such a belief, however misguided, would be evidence that the rapists intended that the women not have Muslim babies for at least as long as they were pregnant with the child that resulted from the rape. Nonetheless, the Court did not even consider the accusations of forced impregnation as measures intended to prevent births, and instead addressed the accusations only in regard to Article II(e): "forcibly transferring children of the group to another group." . . .

A Means of Transferring Children

In her 1996 book, *Rape Warfare: The Hidden Genocide in Bosnia-Herzegovina and Croatia*, Beverly Allen documents how rape and forced pregnancy were a means of transferring children in the Yugoslav conflict: "Pregnant victims are raped consistently until such time as their pregnancies have progressed beyond the possibility of a safe abortion and are then released." The genocidal goal is furthered because "the perpetrator—or the policy according to which he is acting—considers this child to be only Serb and to have none of the identity of the mother."

Of course, classifying rape and forced impregnation as genocide in this way relies on some problematic assumptions. Engle again provides a useful summary of these assumptions:

According to Kalosieh, for example, "Rape was the genocidal strategy"; "forced impregnation at rape camps would serve to increase the Serbian population because '[u]nder Islamic and Muslim law, a child's ethnicity is determined by that of the father.'" [Kelly] Askin makes virtually the same point in her discussion of ethnic cleansing . . . about forcible impregnation with a "different ethnic gene": "'[T]he children of non-Muslim Serbian rapists are not considered to be Muslims.'"

In this narrative, forced impregnation would function to create Serbian babies who, by populating otherwise Muslim territory, would effectively take it over. Rather than forcibly removing the population, Serbs would *change* the Muslim population by ensuring that the next generation was composed of Serbs. [Catharine] MacKinnon stated early on in the war that such was the goal of Serbian rapists of both Croats and Muslims: "Croatian and Muslim women are raped to help make a Serbian state by making Serbian babies."

Siobhán K. Fisher agrees: "For Serbs and Muslims, unlike Jews, the ethnicity of the father is decisive in determining the ethnicity of the child." Allen acknowledges the problematic nature of these assumptions, noting that from a biological standpoint, a zygote resulting from a rape "will contain an equal amount of genetic material from its non-Chetnik, non-Serb mother as it will from its Chetnik or Serb father." The assumption is equally problematic from a cultural standpoint: "Any child produced by such forced impregnation, unless that child is raised by its Serb father in a Serb community, will be assimilated to the cultural, ethnic, religious, national identity of the mother. To call such children 'Chetniks' or 'little Serb soldiers' is clearly a blatant, though highly motivated, stupidity." To say that forced impregnation could in no circumstance result in at least the partial transfer intended by the perpetrators, however, is to deny the biological reality that resulting children take half their genetic material from those perpetrators.

Regardless of the extent to which a rapist's assumptions about identity and genetics are ill-informed, however, what matters from a legal perspective, at least according to the language of the Convention, is the *intent* of the perpetrator. The question, then, is whether the rapist relied on these problematic assumptions in aiming to destroy the group. The fact that such beliefs by "would-be genocidaires" is "blatant, though highly motivated, stupidity" does not remove their actions from the application of the Convention. Unfortunately, this is not the matter the Court addressed. Instead, as it did in addressing claims under section (d), the Court focused on the success of the genocidal design rather than the intent of the perpetrator.

Evidence of Forced Impregnation

Ultimately, the ICJ settled the matter of forced transfer by finding that the evidence "does not establish that there was any form of policy of forced pregnancy, nor that there was any aim to transfer children of the protected group to another group within the meaning of Article II*(e)* of the Convention." Here again, the Court missed or disregarded considerable evidence of forced impregnation. The Court itself acknowledged evidence from *Prosecutor v Kunarac*, in which the ICTY found that, "after raping one of the witnesses, the accused had told her that 'she would now carry a Serb baby and would not know who the father would be.'" The Court left out the context in which that statement was made. The ICTY also had found that [Bosnian Serb military commander Dragoljub] Kunarac "expressed with verbal and physical aggression his view that the rapes against the Muslim women were one of the many ways in which the Serbs could assert their superiority and victory over the Muslims." Additionally, the ICTY found that "[t]he treatment reserved by Dragoljub Kunarac for his victims was motivated by their being Muslims, as is evidenced by the occasions when the accused told the women that they would give birth to Serb babies." The Court failed to address the evidence from the U.S. submission to the U.N. as well, which quoted another witness as stating that while she was being raped, she was told "You should have already left this town. We'll make you have Serbian babies who will be Christians."

The Special Rapporteur of the U.N. Commission on Human Rights endorsed the findings of a special team of medical experts that issued the Mazowiecki Report, finding early in the conflict that "[t]here is clear evidence that Croat, Muslim, and Serb women have been detained for extended periods of time and repeatedly raped." Furthermore, the team found that "[i]n Bosnia and Herzegovina and in Croatia, rape has been used as an instrument of ethnic cleansing." The Special Rapporteur expressed a clear expectation that such rapes would result in pregnancies and birth, stating that a "particular problem arises with regard to the children who have been born, or are expected to be born in the near future, as a result of rape." The Rapporteur went on to discuss necessary measures to provide for the adoption of such children.

The report by the Commission of Experts (as distinguished from the team of medical experts) provides possibly the most concrete evidence of forced impregnation in the context of detention camps:

> [One] pattern of rape involves individuals or groups committing sexual assaults against women for the purpose of terrorizing and humiliating them often as part of the policy of "ethnic cleansing". Survivors of some camps report that they believe they were detained for the purpose of rape. In those camps, all of the women are raped quite frequently, often in front of other internees, and usually accompanied by beatings and torture. Some captors also state that they

are trying to impregnate the women. Pregnant women are detained until it is too late for them to obtain an abortion. One woman was detained by her neighbour (who was a soldier) near her village for six months. She was raped almost daily by three or four soldiers. She was told that she would give birth to a chetnik boy who would kill Muslims when he grew up. They repeatedly said their President had ordered them to do this.

Like the team of medical experts, the Commission explained that these patterns seemed to emerge without regard to ethnicity, stating that "[p]erpetrators tell female victims that they will bear children of the perpetrator's ethnicity, that they must become pregnant, and then hold them in custody until it is too late for the victims to get an abortion." However, "the largest number of alleged perpetrators have [sic] been Bosnian Serbs." Further, while the Commission found that *some* rape and sexual assaults in Bosnia (mostly committed by Serbs against Muslims) were not conducted under "command direction or an overall policy . . . many more seem to be a part of an overall pattern." The Commission found that the evidence of a "large numbers of rapes which occurred in detention centers" especially supported its conclusion that there existed an "overall pattern" if not a policy of rape committed by Serbs against Muslims: "These rapes in detention do not appear to be random, and they indicate at least a policy of encouraging rape."

The evidence above can be summarized as follows: Serbs raped Muslim women with the intent that they become pregnant. At least some of these women were detained in order to force them to carry the pregnancy until it was too late to obtain an abortion. While there is evidence of forced impregnation on all sides of the conflict, only the rape and sexual assault by Serbs against Muslims has been found to be part of an overall pattern, especially with respect to rapes in detention centers. Finally, the ultimate purpose of Serbian detention camps in Bosnia, according to the Commission of Experts, was ethnic cleansing, and the ultimate purpose of many of the rapes, according to the team of medical experts, also was ethnic cleansing.

The relevant question, then, is how forced impregnation can further the goal of "ethnic cleansing" and whether that amounts to a "forcible transfer" under Article II(e)? It would appear that the only way forced impregnation can be classified as ethnic cleansing is if the resulting child is of a different "ethnicity" as that term is defined in reference to "ethnic cleansing." In this case, the evidence points to a policy, or at least a pattern, designed to achieve that end, as well as an intent on the part of some Serbs to achieve that goal. Unfortunately, the Court gave no indication of why it might have found the evidence unpersuasive or, more importantly, whether the legal analysis based on Article II(e) may or may not be sound and why.

The Court's Fears

It is unfortunate that the Court disregarded the allegations that rape and sexual violence constituted acts of genocide, or decided not to acknowledge that acts of sexual violence were committed which could constitute acts of genocide if accompanied by the required specific intent. The Court may have feared the controversy of actually finding a state responsible for such atrocities, recognizing the threat of an international backlash that could have been damaging to the Court. If the Court had acknowledged the occurrence of sexually violent acts that could constitute genocide, it would have had a much harder time denying the evidence of specific intent. Because the evidence demonstrated both a policy of rape and the ultimate aim of ethnic cleansing within Serb detention camps, the Court would have found it difficult to deny the overall pattern evincing the specific intent to destroy the Muslim population. To understand this contention, it is first necessary

Sexual Violence, War, and Bosnia

Although the mass rape campaigns carried out during the war in Bosnia and Herzegovina (1991–95) were created as unprecedented at the time, it is now understood that these were part of a much broader global pattern of war-related violence against women. In conflicts all around the world, women and girls, irrespective of their age, ethnicity, or political affiliation, have been singled out for sexual violence, imprisonment, torture, execution, sexual mutilation, forced pregnancy, rape, and sexual slavery. Acts such as rape, sexual assault, sexual slavery, forced prostitution, forced sterilization, forced abortion, and forced pregnancy may all qualify as crimes under national and international law. Sexual violence is considered to be a war crime, an act of torture, an act of genocide, and a crime against humanity; forced pregnancy (or forced impregnation), recognized as a military strategy used in several conflicts, has been codified under international law as a war crime and a crime against humanity.

The numbers of raped women in the former Yugoslavia vary depending on the sources, ranging from twenty thousand to fifty thousand. While all sides in the Bosnian conflict have committed rapes, Serbian forces appear to have used rape on the largest scale, principally against Muslim women. According to the UN Final Report of the Commission of Experts, the majority of the cases, perpetrated by soldiers, paramilitary groups, local police, as well as civilians, occurred between fall 1991 and the end of 1993.

Joana Daniel-Wrabetz,
in Born of War: Protecting Children of
Sexual Violence Survivors in Conflict Zones, *2007.*

to consider the Court's discussion of ethnic cleansing as distinct from genocide, and second, to apply the Court's evidentiary standard to evaluate why the policy of ethnic cleansing is "indicative of the presence of a specific intent."

As noted earlier, the Commission of Experts determined that ethnic cleansing was the ultimate purpose behind the Bosnian Serb detention camps. According to the Court, "the term 'ethnic cleansing' has no *legal* significance of its own." Ethnic cleansing is the process of "rendering an area ethnically homogenous by using force or intimidation to remove persons of given groups from the area." In this sense, ethnic cleansing is not necessarily the same as genocide. For example, government forces may post notices threatening to punish all members of an ethnic minority (or other protected group) who do not leave a specific region within a given timeframe. The forces may even commit random acts of violence against the civilian population in order to terrorize the minority group enough so that they will leave. If, however, the government forces permit the minority group to leave and evince no intent to destroy, but only to relocate the group, the acts do not constitute genocide, although they may violate other international norms. As the Court noted, however, "[t]his is not to say that acts described as 'ethnic cleansing' may never constitute genocide, if they are such as to be characterized as [among the categories of acts prohibited by Article II] of the Convention, provided such action is carried out with the necessary specific intent. . . ." Most importantly, the Court declared that "it is clear that acts of 'ethnic cleansing' may occur in parallel to acts prohibited by Article II of the Convention, and *may be significant as indicative of the presence of a specific intent . . . inspiring those acts.*"

Recalling the evidence of a policy of rape within Bosnian Serb detention camps, Bosnia could have argued that the policy of rape in the context of a campaign of ethnic cleansing constituted a pattern of acts that together indicated the specific intent of genocide. The Court held that in order for a pattern of acts to indicate specific intent, the pattern "would have to be such that it could only point to the existence of such intent." Where the court found that the *actus reus* [guilty act] of genocide had occurred, it also found that Bosnia had "not established the existence of [specific intent] on the part of the Respondent, either on the basis of a concerted plan, or on the basis that the events reviewed . . . reveal a consistent pattern of conduct *which could only point to the existence of such intent.*"

In the case of rape, it is hard to see what intent, other than destruction, the policy could implicate. It might be argued that rape is often an incident of war. A canvassing of academic literature would provide multiple psychological and sociological explanations for individual instances of rape revolving around issues of power and organized violence. However, such explanations would not fit within the evidence of a calculated *policy* of rape, particularly as part of an ethnic cleansing goal. In addressing ethnic cleansing in Bosnia, Allen proposes that that rape was used as a method of terrorizing populations into leaving:

> Chetniks or other Serb forces enter a Bosnian-Herzegovinian or Croatian village, take several women of varying ages from their homes, rape them in public view, and depart. The news of this atrocious event spreads rapidly through the village. Several days later, regular Bosnian Serb soldiers or Serb soldiers from the Yugoslav Army arrive and offer the now-terrified residents safe passage away from the village on the condition they never return.

This provides an example of how rape may be used in a campaign of non-genocidal ethnic cleansing. However, this explanation fails to account for the policy of rape in detention camps in which the targeted population is deliberately prevented from leaving.

The evidence of forced impregnation, with the intent of some to force Muslim women to have "Serbian" babies, in an environment of detention centers where the ultimate purpose was to bring about ethnic cleansing, can only point to the existence of an intent to destroy Muslims. Rape was used with the intent of achieving "ethnic cleansing" by destroying the Muslim population. By preventing births of Muslim children and forcing the births of (in the opinion of the attacker) non-Muslim children, the regions were to be "cleansed" of Muslims. No matter how unlikely the attackers' ultimate success would prove to be, the evidence shows that the rapes were prohibited by multiple sections of Article II of the Convention, and that, in committing these acts, at least some of the attackers had a specific intent to destroy the group. In this regard, Serb forces used the rape of Muslims in Bosnia as a tool of genocide. However, even if the Court had made such a determination, there still would remain the issue of attribution. The Court's refusal to identify the *actus reus* of genocide based on a policy of rape and ethnic cleansing, along with its refusal to recognize the genocidal intent that necessarily follows, creates considerable ambiguity concerning the status of sexual violence, forced impregnation, and the prevention of births under the Convention.

Rape and Denying Genocide

The ICJ simply was not willing to foreclose the *possibility* of holding a state responsible for genocide. At the same time, however, it was not prepared to attribute responsibility to Serbia. In general, the Court recognized ongoing state responsibility under the Convention as a matter of international law while setting a high standard of proof for establishing genocidal intent, thus avoiding a holding that Serbia was responsible by holding that the burden had not been satisfied. This was possible because most acts in war that could constitute the *actus reus* of genocide can fairly easily be attributed to non-genocidal intent. For example, a belligerent in war may justify killing or causing bodily and mental harm through means such as torture by reference to some military objective. For rape and other sexual and reproductive violent acts performed as part of a policy of ethnic cleansing in Bosnia, however, it would have been far more difficult to find a non-genocidal intent, particularly with regard to those camps established for the sole purpose of holding women for rape and sexual violence. Because the mental element could not be easily denied, and because the Court wanted to avoid finding an occurrence of genocide possibly attributable to Serbia, the Court had to avoid the mental question altogether. This could only be accomplished by disregarding the evidence of rape and sexual violence, which alone may constitute the *actus reus* of genocide. In the end, this led the Court to ignore considerable evidence of such acts and resulted in a further muddling of the already unclear legal status of rape as genocide under international law.

"Male sexual violence is a component of wars all over the world, . . . [but] only 3% of [relief organizations] mentioned the experience of men in their literature."

Rape of Men Is Often Unacknowledged During Genocide

Will Storr

Will Storr is a novelist and long-form journalist whose work has appeared in British newspapers such as the Telegraph *and the* Observer, *as well as magazines such as* Esquire. *In the following viewpoint, he discusses widespread rape and sexual violence against men and boys during the war and violence in Uganda. He argues that rape of men is present in conflicts throughout the world, but it is rarely discussed because male victims are ashamed to come forward. Storr adds that aid agencies often ignore sexual violence against men, and seem reluctant to discuss it for fear that there will be fewer resources to help female victims of sexual violence.*

As you read, consider the following questions:

1. In which conflicts did Lara Stemple find evidence of sexual violence against men, according to Storr?

2. What does Salome Atim say wives often do when they discover their husbands have been raped, as reported by the author?

3. According to Dr. Angella Ntinda in Uganda, as cited by Storr, what percentage of men referred to her from the Refugee Law Project (RLP) are victims of sexual violence?

Of all the secrets of war, there is one that is so well kept that it exists mostly as a rumour. It is usually denied by the perpetrator and his victim. Governments, aid agencies and human rights defenders at the UN barely acknowledge its possibility. Yet every now and then someone gathers the courage to tell of it. This is just what happened on an ordinary afternoon in the office of a kind and careful counsellor in Kampala, Uganda. For four years Eunice Owiny had been employed by Makerere University's Refugee Law Project (RLP) to help displaced people from all over Africa work through their traumas. This particular case, though, was a puzzle. A female client was having marital difficulties. "My husband can't have sex," she complained. "He feels very bad about this. I'm sure there's something he's keeping from me."

"It Happened to Me"

Owiny invited the husband in. For a while they got nowhere. Then Owiny asked the wife to leave. The man then murmured cryptically: "It happened to me." Owiny frowned. He reached into his pocket and pulled out an old sanitary pad. "Mama Eunice," he said. "I am in pain. I have to use this."

Laying the pus-covered pad on the desk in front of him, he gave up his secret. During his escape from the civil war in neighbouring Congo, he had been separated from his wife and taken by rebels. His captors raped him, three times a day, every day for three years. And he wasn't the only one. He watched as man after man was taken and raped. The wounds of one were so grievous that he died in the cell in front of him.

"That was hard for me to take," Owiny tells me today. "There are certain things you just don't believe can happen to a man, you get me? But I know now that sexual violence against men is a huge problem. Everybody has heard the women's stories. But nobody has heard the men's."

It's not just in East Africa that these stories remain unheard. One of the few academics to have looked into the issue in any detail is Lara Stemple, of the University of California's Health and Human Rights Law Project. Her study *Male Rape and Human Rights* notes incidents of male sexual violence as a weapon of wartime or political aggression in countries such as Chile, Greece, Croatia, Iran, Kuwait, the former Soviet Union and the former Yugoslavia. Twenty-one per cent of Sri Lankan males who were seen at a London torture treatment centre reported sexual abuse while in detention. In El Salvador, 76% of male political prisoners surveyed in the 1980s described at least one incidence of sexual torture. A study of 6,000 concentration-camp inmates in Sarajevo [in the former Yugoslavia] found that 80% of men reported having been raped.

I've come to Kampala to hear the stories of the few brave men who have agreed to speak to me: a rare opportunity to find out about a controversial and deeply taboo issue. In Uganda, survivors are at risk of arrest by police, as they are likely to assume that they're gay—a crime in this country and in 38 of the 53 African nations. They will probably be ostracised by friends, rejected by family and turned away by the UN and the myriad international NGOs [nongovernmental organizations] that are equipped, trained and ready to help women. They are wounded, isolated and in danger. In the words of Owiny: "They are despised."

But they are willing to talk, thanks largely to the RLP's British director, Dr Chris Dolan. Dolan first heard of wartime sexual violence against men in the late 1990s while researching his PhD in northern Uganda, and he sensed that the problem might be dramatically underestimated. Keen to gain a fuller grasp of its depth and nature, he put up posters throughout Kampala in June 2009 announcing a "workshop" on the issue in a local school. On the day, 150 men arrived. In a burst of candour, one attendee admitted: "It's happened to all of us here." It soon became known among Uganda's 200,000-strong refugee population that the RLP were helping men who had been raped during conflict. Slowly, more victims began to come forward.

I meet Jean Paul on the hot, dusty roof of the RLP's HQ in Old Kampala. He wears a scarlet high-buttoned shirt and holds himself with his neck lowered, his eyes cast towards the ground, as if in apology for his impressive height. He has a prominent upper lip that shakes continually—a nervous condition that makes him appear as if he's on the verge of tears.

Jean Paul was at university in Congo, studying electronic engineering, when his father—a wealthy businessman—was accused by the army of aiding the enemy and shot dead. Jean Paul fled in January 2009, only to be abducted by rebels. Along with six other men and six women he was marched to a forest in the Virunga National Park.

Later that day, the rebels and their prisoners met up with their cohorts who were camped out in the woods. Small camp fires could be seen here and there between the shadowy ranks of trees. While the women were sent off to prepare food and coffee, 12 armed fighters surrounded the men. From his place on the ground, Jean Paul looked up to see the commander leaning over them. In his 50s, he was bald, fat and in military uniform. He wore a red bandana around his neck and had strings of leaves tied around his elbows.

"You are all spies," the commander said. "I will show you how we punish spies." He pointed to Jean Paul. "Remove your clothes and take a position like a Muslim man."

"I Cannot Do These Things"

Jean Paul thought he was joking. He shook his head and said: "I cannot do these things."

The commander called a rebel over. Jean Paul could see that he was only about nine years old. He was told, "Beat this man and remove this clothes." The boy attacked him with his gun butt. Eventually, Jean Paul begged: "Okay, okay. I will take off my clothes." Once naked, two rebels held him in a kneeling position with his head pushed towards the earth.

At this point, Jean Paul breaks off. The shaking in his lip more pronounced than ever, he lowers his head a little further and says: "I am sorry for the things I am going to say now." The commander put his left hand on the back of his skull and used his right to beat him on the backside "like a horse". Singing a witch doctor song, and with everybody watching, the commander then began. The moment he started, Jean Paul vomited.

Eleven rebels waited in a queue and raped Jean Paul in turn. When he was too exhausted to hold himself up, the next attacker would wrap his arm under Jean Paul's hips and lift him by the stomach. He bled freely: "Many, many, many bleeding," he says, "I could feel it like water." Each of the male prisoners was raped 11 times that night and every night that followed.

On the ninth day, they were looking for firewood when Jean Paul spotted a huge tree with roots that formed a small grotto of shadows. Seizing his moment, he crawled in and watched, trembling, as the rebel guards searched for him. After five hours of watching their feet as they hunted for him, he listened as they came up with a plan: they would let off a round of gunfire and tell the commander that Jean Paul had been killed. Eventually he emerged, weak from his ordeal and his diet of only two bananas per day during his captivity. Dressed only in his underpants, he crawled through the undergrowth "slowly, slowly, slowly, slowly, like a snake" back into town.

Today, despite his hospital treatment, Jean Paul still bleeds when he walks. Like many victims, the wounds are such that he's supposed to restrict his diet to soft foods such as bananas, which are expensive, and Jean Paul can only afford maize and millet. His brother keeps asking what's wrong with him. "I don't want to tell him," says Jean Paul. "I fear he will say: 'Now, my brother is not a man.'"

A Conspiracy of Silence

It is for this reason that both perpetrator and victim enter a conspiracy of silence and why male survivors often find, once their story is discovered, that they lose the support and comfort of those around them. In the patriarchal societies found in many developing countries, gender roles are strictly defined.

"In Africa no man is allowed to be vulnerable," says RLP's gender officer Salome Atim. "You have to be masculine, strong. You should never break down or cry. A man must be a leader and provide for the whole family. When he fails to reach that set standard, society perceives that there is something wrong."

Often, she says, wives who discover their husbands have been raped decide to leave them. "They ask me: 'So now how am I going to live with him? As what? Is this still a husband? Is it a wife?' They ask, 'If he can be raped, who is protecting me?' There's one family I have been working closely with in which the husband has been raped twice. When his wife discovered this, she went home, packed her belongings, picked up their child and left. Of course that brought down this man's heart."

Back at RLP I'm told about the other ways in which their clients have been made to suffer. Men aren't simply raped, they are forced to penetrate holes in banana trees that run with acidic sap, to sit with their genitals over a fire, to drag rocks tied to their penis, to give oral sex to queues of soldiers, to be penetrated with screwdrivers and sticks. Atim has now seen so many male survivors that, frequently, she can spot them the moment they sit down. "They tend to lean forward and will often sit on one buttock," she tells me. "When they cough, they grab their lower regions. At times, they will stand up and there's blood on the chair. And they often have some kind of smell."

Because there has been so little research into the rape of men during war, it's not possible to say with any certainty why it happens or even how common it is—although a rare 2010 survey, published in the *Journal of the American Medical Association*, found that 22% of men and 30% of women in Eastern Congo reported conflict-related sexual violence. As for Atim, she says: "Our staff are overwhelmed by the cases we've got, but in terms of actual numbers? This is the tip of the iceberg."

Later on I speak with Dr Angella Ntinda, who treats referrals from the RLP. She tells me: "Eight out of 10 patients from RLP will be talking about some sort of sexual abuse."

"Eight out of 10 men?" I clarify.

"No. Men *and* women," she says.

"What about men?"

"I think all the men."

I am aghast.

"*All* of them?" I say.

"Yes," she says. "All the men."

Failing the Victims

The research by Lara Stemple at the University of California doesn't only show that male sexual violence is a component of wars all over the world, it also suggests that international aid organisations are failing male victims. Her study cites a review of 4,076 NGOs that have addressed wartime sexual violence. Only 3% of them mentioned the experience of men in their literature. "Typically," Stemple says, "as a passing reference."

On my last night I arrive at the house of Chris Dolan. We're high on a hill, watching the sun go down over the neighbourhoods of Salama Road and Luwafu, with Lake Victoria in the far distance. As the air turns from blue to mauve to black, a muddled galaxy of white, green and orange bulbs flickers on; a pointillist accident spilled over distant valleys and hills. A magnificent hubbub rises from it all. Babies screaming, children playing, cicadas, chickens, songbirds, cows, televisions and, floating above it all, the call to prayer at a distant mosque.

Stemple's findings on the failure of aid agencies is no surprise to Dolan. "The organisations working on sexual and gender-based violence don't talk about it," he says. "It's systematically silenced. If you're very, very lucky they'll give it a tangential mention at the end of a report. You might get five seconds of: 'Oh and men can also be the victims of sexual violence.' But there's no data, no discussion."

As part of an attempt to correct this, the RLP produced a documentary in 2010 called *Gender Against Men*. When it was screened, Dolan says that attempts were made to stop him. "Were these attempts by people in well-known, international aid agencies?" I ask.

"Yes," he replies. "There's a fear among them that this is a zero-sum game; that there's a pre-defined cake and if you start talking about men, you're going to somehow eat a chunk of this cake that's taken them a long time to bake." Dolan points to a November 2006 UN report that followed an international conference on sexual violence in this area of East Africa.

"I know for a fact that the people behind the report insisted the definition of rape be restricted to women," he says, adding that one of the RLP's donors, Dutch Oxfam, refused to provide any more funding unless he'd promise that 70% of his client base was female. He also recalls a man whose case was "particularly bad" and was referred to the UN's refugee agency, the UNHCR. "They told him: 'We have a programme for vulnerable women, but not men.'"

It reminds me of a scene described by Eunice Owiny: "There is a married couple," she said. "The man has been raped, the woman has been raped. Disclosure is easy for the woman. She gets the medical treatment, she gets the attention, she's supported by so many organisations. But the man is inside, dying."

"In a nutshell, that's exactly what happens," Dolan agrees. "Part of the activism around women's rights is: 'Let's prove that women are as good as men.' But the other side is you should look at the fact that men can be weak and vulnerable."

Leaving Out Men

Margot Wallström, the UN special representative of the secretary-general for sexual violence in conflict, insists in a statement that the UNHCR extends its services to refugees of both genders. But she concedes that the "great stigma" men face suggests that the real number of survivors is higher than that reported. Wallström says the focus remains on women because they are "overwhelmingly" the victims. Nevertheless, she adds, "we do know of many cases of men and boys being raped."

But when I contact Stemple by email, she describes a "constant drum beat that women are *the* rape victims" and a milieu in which men are treated as a "monolithic perpetrator class".

"International human rights law leaves out men in nearly all instruments designed to address sexual violence," she continues. "The UN Security Council Resolution 1325 in 2000 treats wartime sexual violence as something that only impacts on women and girls. . . . Secretary of State Hillary Clinton recently announced $44m [million] to implement this resolution. Because of its entirely exclusive focus on female victims, it seems unlikely that any of these new funds will reach the thousands of men and boys who suffer from this kind of abuse. Ignoring male rape not only neglects men, it also harms women by reinforcing a viewpoint that equates 'female' with 'victim', thus hampering our ability to see women as strong and empowered. In the same way, silence about male victims reinforces unhealthy expectations about men and their supposed invulnerability."

Considering Dolan's finding that "female rape is significantly underreported and male rape almost never", I ask Stemple if, following her research, she believes it might be a hitherto unimagined part of all wars. "No one knows, but I do think it's safe to say that it's likely that it's been a part of many wars throughout history and that taboo has played a part in the silence."

As I leave Uganda, there's a detail of a story that I can't forget. Before receiving help from the RLP, one man went to see his local doctor. He told him he had been raped four times, that he was injured and depressed and his wife had threatened to leave him. The doctor gave him a Panadol [an over-the-counter pain medicine similar to Tylenol].

| "*Sexual abuse was a significant component [of the Holocaust].*"

Violence Against Women Was an Important Part of the Holocaust

Rochelle Saidel

Rochelle Saidel is founder and executive director of Remember the Women Institute and the coeditor of Sexual Violence Against Jewish Women During the Holocaust. *In the following viewpoint, she argues that sexual violence against women was widespread during the Holocaust. This violence included everything from rape used as a weapon of terror and humiliation by German soldiers to situations in which Jewish women were forced to provide sex to "rescuers" who agreed to shield them from the Nazis. Saidel says that sexual violence has sometimes been ignored in Holocaust discussions, perhaps because of shame. She argues that these incidents need to be uncovered and brought into the open.*

As you read, consider the following questions:

1. Though the exact numbers of sexual violations during the Holocaust cannot be known, what does Saidel say can be known?

Rochelle Saidel, "Time to Talk About Sexual Violence During the Holocaust," *Times of Israel*, December 19, 2012. www.rememberwomen.org. Copyright © 2012 by Rochelle Saidel. All rights reserved. Reproduced by permission.

2. Besides shame, what other reason does Saidel say is sometimes given for not discussing sexual violence during the Holocaust?

3. How has the status of rape as a war crime changed since the Nuremberg trials, according to the author?

The tenth day of the Hebrew month of Tevet, which is December 23 this year [2012], is designated as the *yartzeit* (memorial anniversary) for Holocaust victims whose date of death is unknown. Since many victims of sexual violence were subsequently murdered on indeterminable dates, this is an appropriate time to talk about rape and other forms of sexual abuse during the Holocaust. As in other genocides, during the Holocaust the persecution of women and girls (and some men and boys) included sexual violence. Even though we cannot ever know the exact numbers, it is an indisputable fact that Jewish women and girls were sexually violated.

Documented Sexual Violence

Rape and sexual violence in connection with later genocides have been well documented, and in these cases victims have come forward. Some experts even believe that an open discussion about sexual violence during the Holocaust might have alerted us to its recurrence in later genocides. Likewise, now that these atrocities during later genocides have been widely exposed, analyzed, publicized, and in some cases brought to justice, perhaps Holocaust victims will be motivated to come forward.

There are victim and witness testimonies about rape during the Holocaust, in roundups, in ghettos, in resistance movements, in concentration camps, death camps, and slave labor camps. Virtually all women inducted into camps were sexually abused by being forced to stand naked in front of men, and by having their vaginas poked, prodded, and smeared with caustic disinfectant. Sometimes soldiers in the *Einsatzgruppen*

[Nazi death squads] who shot Jews into pits in the East first raped young women. Others were forced into prostitution in bordellos or the private homes of soldiers or guards. Some women were murdered and their bodies then sexually violated. And girls and women saved in hiding by non-Jewish "rescuers" sometimes had to pay with their bodies. In other settings, women were forced to provide sex for food and their means of survival, also a form of rape. Occasionally a Nazi-appointed Jewish governing council in a ghetto (*Judenrat*) had to furnish Nazis with pretty young women to (temporarily) prevent the general population's deportation.

Silence and Shame

With all of this evidence, it seems that an accounting of sexual violence would be part of the general history of the Holocaust. Instead, the subject has hardly been discussed. While included in some memoirs, especially early ones, sexual abuse is almost never mentioned in historians' accounts. Holocaust memorial museums have also avoided the subject. One cited excuse for dismissing the rape of Jewish women is the Nazi *Rassenschande* law. But this law, which prohibited sexual relations between so-called Aryans and Jews, was about consensual sex. And even if it had been about rape, do today's laws prevent rape?

One real but unwarranted reason for the silence is shame, or *shanda* in Yiddish (with the same root as that of the second half of the German *Rassenschande*—here, literally shaming the race). Some victims who broke their silence have asked that their violation remain a secret. However, no victim of rape (or her family) should be ashamed. The shame always belongs to the perpetrator, despite some cultures' inclination to blame the victim. Is it because of the shame factor that most Holocaust institutions and scholars have chosen to ignore or at best marginalize the issue of sexual violence?

Another baseless reason for excising sexual violation from Holocaust history is that including it would detract from the narrative of the totality of the Holocaust. However, sexual abuse was a significant component, and we can more fully understand the Holocaust only by examining all components. Scholars study what happened in every individual country, city, ghetto, or camp, and, unfortunately, sexual violation is also a component of the comprehensive history of the Holocaust.

While Nazis and their collaborators were not officially ordered to rape, it does not follow that rape and sexual abuse of Jewish women and girls did not take place. Nor does it follow that sexual abuse was not used to humiliate them. Based on witness reports, rapes often resulted in the murder of the victims. Although not considered a war crime during the Nuremberg war criminal trials [held in 1945–1946], today rape during the Holocaust would fall within the definition of crimes against humanity.

In November 2012, a historic symposium was convened by the USC [University of Southern California] Shoah ["Holocaust"] Foundation and Remember the Women Institute. This groundbreaking international meeting of scholars and human rights experts, focusing specifically on sexual violence during the Holocaust, was prompted by the publication of *Sexual Violence Against Jewish Women During the Holocaust* (eds. Hedgepeth and Saidel 2010). One result of the symposium is the participants' decision to heighten efforts to find victims and witnesses willing to talk about their experiences. Time is running out, but we believe it is still possible to find and record testimonies about sexual violence during the Holocaust.

Periodical and Internet Sources Bibliography

The following articles have been selected to supplement the diverse views presented in this chapter.

David Buchanan   "Gendercide and Human Rights," *Journal of Genocide Research*, 2002.

Kimberley A. Ducey   "Dilemmas of Teaching the 'Greatest Silence': Rape-as-Genocide in Rwanda, Darfur, and Congo," *Genocide Studies and Prevention*, November 19, 2010.

Maureen Hiebert   "'Too Many Cides' to Gendercide Studies?," H-Net Reviews, September 2005. www .h-net.org.

Georgina Holmes   "'Living on Gold Should Be a Blessing; Instead It Is a Curse: Mass Rape and Genocide by Attrition in the Democratic Republic of the Congo," *RUSI Journal*, vol. 157, no. 6, 2012.

Anne Manne   "Gendercide," *The Monthly*, June 2010.

Emily Rauhala   "Rape as a Weapon of War: Men Suffer Too," *Time*, August 3, 2011.

Robin May Schott   "War Rape, Natality, and Genocide," *Journal of Genocide Research*, vol. 13, nos. 1–2, 2011.

Laura Sjoberg   "Gendered Experiences of Genocide: Anfal Survivors in Kurdistan-Iraq," *Gender & Development*, vol. 20, no. 1, 2012.

Nandini Sundar   "Nationbuilding, Gender and War Crimes in South Asia," *Journal of Genocide Research*, vol. 14, no. 2, 2012.

Vahé Tachijan   "Gender, Nationalism, Exclusion: The Reintegration Process of Female Survivors of the Armenian Genocide," *Nations and Nationalism*, January 14, 2009.

CHAPTER 4

Who Is the Target of Gendercide?

Chapter Preface

One of the most notorious single acts of gendercide occurred in Canada on December 6, 1989. On that date, a twenty-five-year-old man named Marc Lépine shot and killed fourteen women and wounded ten others at the École Polytechnique, the School of Engineering at the University of Montreal.

Lépine targeted women specifically because he was angry about gains women had made in nontraditional roles, such as in engineering. He apparently blamed these advances, and women's greater presence in universities, for the fact that the School of Engineering had rejected him for admission. As quoted by Adam Jones on the Gendercide Watch website, Lépine's suicide note declared, "The feminists always have a talent for enraging me. They want to retain the advantages of being women . . . while trying to grab those of men."

Some in Canada were initially reluctant to see Lépine's act in a political or gendercidal context. His suicide note was not released, and some characterized him as a madman who had committed a random act of violence. Others have emphasized the specifically antifeminist and misogynist nature of the killings. For example, Francine Pelletier, a feminist activist and writer, was quoted by Julie Bindel in a December 3, 2012, article in Britain's *Guardian* newspaper as saying, "I always felt those women died in my name. Some of them probably weren't even feminist, they just had the nerve to believe they were peers, not subordinates of their male classmates."

Since the massacre, Canada has declared December 6 a national day of commemoration. The event sparked movements to raise awareness of violence against women and also inspired gun-control legislation. Lépine failed in his goal of reducing women in the professions. In the decade after the massacre, the number of women on engineering faculties more than doubled, to nine thousand. Feminist writer Andrea Dworkin declared, "It is incumbent upon each of us to be the woman that Marc Lépine wanted to kill. We must live with this honour, this courage. We must drive out fear. We must hold on. We must create. We must resist."

The viewpoints in this chapter looks at other targets of gendercidal violence, including women, men, and so-called third genders.

"A growing number of women activists. . .are intensifying their own fight
against the killings and the patriarchal
system that still grips Turkish family
life."

Islamic Culture Targets Women for Gendercide

Alexander Christie-Miller

Alexander Christie-Miller is a correspondent for the Christian
Science Monitor. *In the following viewpoint, he argues that the
clash of conservative values along with rapid modernization is
causing a rise in honor killings in Turkey. Christie-Miller explains that some citizens compare the rise of honor killings to a
gendocide of women, and points to concerns that the government
is not doing enough to stop the trend. While the government has
passed laws to address the problem, many do not see the laws
being applied.*

As you read, consider the following questions:

1. Where was Turkey ranked on the World Economic
   Forum's Global Gender Gap?

2. What evidence may some cite to argue that Turkey's laws created to fight female violence and honor killings are not working?

3. What comment did Turkey's prime minister make that upset many women activists, according to Christie-Miller?

A drastic rise in reported "honor" killings and fatal domestic violence in Turkey has sparked a vigorous debate about the government's recent attempts to address the problem. It also highlights the clash of conservative values with the country's rapid modernization.

Government figures released in February suggest murders of women increased 14-fold in seven years, from 66 in 2002, to 953 in the first seven months of 2009. In the past seven months, one rights organization has compiled more than 264 cases—nearly one per day—reported in the press in which a woman was killed by a family member, husband, ex-husband, or partner.

"There's been an incredible increase," says Gulhan Yag, a young activist who recently attended a funeral for a teenage girl killed for eloping with her boyfriend. "This feels like a genocide against women."

Amidst a surge of public outrage, the Islam-rooted ruling party is being cast as both villain and hero. While some argue it has fueled social conservatism, others claim that for the first time, a problem that has long plagued Turkish family life is finally being uncovered—in part because women are asserting their rights and drawing attention to the issue.

"We know that violence against women has been a long-standing bleeding wound of the society," Prime Minister Recep Tayyip Erdogan told a convention last month on the eve of International Women's Day. "It is being reflected by the media as a growing issue when it is simply the hidden and unspoken truths being uncovered."

On Paper, Progress for Women

On paper at least, Mr. Erdogan's government has an impressive record for fighting the problem.

Since 2006, police officers have undergone training to combat violence against women, and now a specialized domestic violence police unit is being set up. Penal and civil codes were changed in 2004 and 2005 to increase sentences for honor killers.

Meanwhile, amendments to the family protection law currently in parliament will for the first time allow judges to impose restraining orders in relation to non-married couples.

"More women know their rights, people are more aware than before, and for the last five years police have been trained in these issues," says Meltem Agduk, United Nations Population Program Coordinator for Turkey.

Are Police Willing to Help?

But others question both the effectiveness of the legislation, and the government's own commitment to the problem.

"Laws have been made but they are not being applied," says Canan Gullu, chairwoman of the Turkish Association of Women's Federations. "Police stations don't work as they should and there are not enough safe houses for women."

The government passed a law in 2005 recommending that municipalities with more than 50,000 people should have a women's shelter. Few have paid attention to the vaguely worded, noncompulsory legislation, and so far only 65 are operating, compared to the 1,400 that would exist with proper implementation.

Activists claim police are unwilling or unable to help vulnerable women. In February, Arzu Yildirim, a mother of two, was murdered, allegedly by her ex-boyfriend after having requests for police protection rejected. Hers was one among many similar cases.

The funeral Ms. Yag attended was for 19-year-old Hatice Firat, who was killed Feb. 28 after running away to live with her boyfriend—an offense her relatives saw as staining the family's honor. Local media said her brother was the prime suspect.

But her case was not without sympathy. Yag and a group of other women arranged for a funeral after Firat's family refused to pick up her body. And a crowd of 150 people bore her coffin through the streets of the southeastern Turkish city of Mersin chanting slogans against the murder of women.

Police detained 11 relatives as well as her boyfriend, and two days later, 22 members of Parliament urged the government to investigate the reason for the rise in women's murders.

Prime Minister's Comment Draws Ire

Some see the government as part of the problem, however, claiming that the Islamic values espoused by Turkey's leaders have fueled the violence. Erdogan particularly drew the ire of women's activists last year when he said at a conference in Istanbul that he "did not believe" in gender equality, a comment that was widely reported in Turkish news outlets. (He went on to say that "that's why I prefer to say 'equal opportunity.' Men and women are different in nature, they complete each other.")

"If our prime minister says men and women aren't equal, it affects men. There's no positive example for them. They are now thinking that they can do anything they want," says Gulsun Kanat, a volunteer social worker for the women's charity Mor Cati.

Though it is impossible to substantiate such claims, Turkey's statistics on gender equality remain abysmal by almost any standard. While in recent years the country has made tremendous strides economically, improved the situation of its ethnic and religious minorities, and is increasingly enjoying greater political clout on the global stage, it has lan-

Are Honor Killings Permissible?

Percent of Muslims who say that honor killings are never justified when . . .

	Male committed the offense	Female committed the offense	Difference
Southern-Eastern Europe			
Russia	67	60	+7*
Albania	68	67	+1
Bosnia-Herzegovina	79	79	0
Kosovo	60	61	-1
Central Asia			
Azerbaijan	86	82	+4
Kazakhstan	84	84	0
Tajikistan	49	49	0
Turkey	68	68	0
Kyrgyzstan	55	58	-3
Uzbekistan	46	60	-14*
Southeast Asia			
Indonesia	82	82	0
Malaysia	59	59	0
Thailand**	50	52	-2

(Continued)

*Statistically significant differences.
**Interviews conducted with Muslims in five southern provinces only.

TAKEN FROM: "The World's Muslims: Religion, Politics and Society," The Pew Forum on Religion and Public Life, April 30, 2013, p. 89. www .pewforum.org.

Are Honor Killings Permissible? (continued)

Percent of Muslims who say that honor killings are never justified when ...

	Male committed the offense	Female committed the offense	Difference
South Asia			
Bangladesh	38	34	+4
Pakistan	48	45	+3
Afghanistan	24	24	0
Middle East North-Africa			
Jordan	81	34	+47*
Iraq	33	22	+11*
Egypt	41	31	+10*
Lebanon	55	45	+10
Tunisia	62	57	+5
Palestinian territory	46	44	+2
Morocco	64	65	-1

*Statistically significant differences.

TAKEN FROM: "The World's Muslims: Religion, Politics and Society," The Pew Forum on Religion and Public Life, April 30, 2013, p. 89. www.pewforum.org.

guished near the bottom of the World Economic Forum's Global Gender Gap reports since the index was created in 2005. It is currently ranked 126 out of 134 countries—lower even than Iran.

On the question of the rising violence, some suggest the rapid urbanization of the past two decades, twinned with the growth of civil society movements, have given rise to a gender war.

"A lot of the honor killings in Istanbul are being committed by people who moved from villages in the southeast," says Vildan Yirmibesoglu, head of Istanbul's Human Rights Council. "Women who didn't previously go out on the streets are part of community life in a way they didn't used to be. They want to study to go to school and to express themselves, and families don't approve of this."

Meanwhile, a growing number of women activists like those who buried Hatice Firat are intensifying their own fight against the killings and the patriarchal system that still grips Turkish family life.

"Men killed her, and we didn't allow men to bury her," says Yag, whose fellow activists carried out the funeral rites traditionally performed by mosque officials. "I'm at a point now where I draw power from the fact that I know we have to fight against this crime."

"Honor killings normally target the women-folk . . . but in some cases . . . men kill or maim other men for reasons related to family 'honor.'"

Honor Killings of Muslim Males in the West

Daniel Pipes

Daniel Pipes is a historian, writer, political commentator, as well as the president of the Middle East Forum. In the following viewpoint, he argues that women are not the only victims of honor killings. Pipes says it is not uncommon for men to kill or maim other men for reasons related to family honor. He points to several cases where men have been killed or severely injured because of relationships viewed as improper with a female relative. Pipes says there have also been cases of men killing or injuring another man because he was a homosexual or viewed as having feminine traits.

As you read, consider the following questions:

1. Why was it seen as unusual that a young man was murdered for impregnating a girl, and not the girl?

2. What is the Islamic doctrine of *kafa'a*?

3. Why is a Muslim man who displays feminine traits at risk of being injured or killed?

Islamic honor killings normally target the women-folk, bearers of the family honor (*'ird*), not the men involved with them. But in some cases, to be documented here, men kill or maim other men for reasons related to family "honor."

Gets girl pregnant, her lover murdered by her relatives: A Bangladeshi father and his two teenage sons were just found guilty of an honor killing in Oxford, England. What makes the case unusual is that Chomir Ali, 44, ordered Mohammed Mujibar Rahman, 19, and Mamnoor Rahman, 16, to kill not his daughter and their sister, Manna Begum, but the 19-year-old Iranian Muslim boy who made her pregnant, Arash Ghorbani-Zarin. This horrid incident (Ghorbani-Zarin was stabbed 46 times, mostly in the chest) brings Italy to mind rather than the Muslim world, where the pregnant daughter/ sister would usually be the victim. (November 5, 2005) *Dec. 13, 2005 update:* At sentencing today, Chomir Ali got a minimum of 20 years in jail, Mohammed Mujibar Rahman got a minimum of 16 years, and Mamnoor Rahman a minimum of 14 years for their parts in the murder.

Preventing marriage to an unworthy bride: Rachid (30) and Mohamed (33) and a brother-in-law, Ali (31), tried to abduct their brother/brother-in-law on his wedding day in Brussels and spirit him off to Morocco, their ancestral country. They took these steps because they considered his bride unworthy, the prosecution asserted. (Although of Moroccan origin, the girl had Spanish citizenship.) Failing in this, during the wedding ceremony on July 5, they dealt the bridegroom several blows and tried to tie him down to force him into their car. The wedding party members intervened, prevented the abduction, and called the police, who arrested the trio. *Comment:* The Islamic doctrine of *kafa'a*, requires that the bridegroom be socially on a par with his bride, not the reverse, so this case comes as as a surprise. (July 7, 2008)

Fiancé killed by intended's brother in Canada: As Feroz Mangal and Khatera Sadiqi, 23 and 20, sat in a car on Sep. 19, 2006, they were shot by Khatera's brother Hasibullah Sadiqi, 23. He killed them because Khatera decided to marry without her father's permission and then moved into the house of Feroz' family before their wedding. Almost three years later, he has been found guilty of two counts of first-degree murder and sentenced to life in prison with no chance of parole for 25 years. (May 31, 2009)

Man attacked with acid for relationship with a married woman: A Danish man of Asian origin, 24, is in a critical condition after an attack by four men about 2 a.m. on July 2 in Marchant Road, Leytonstone, east London, due to his having "insulted" a religious family by developing a close relationship with a married woman. The assailants poured sulphuric acid on his face and down his throat, stabbed him twice in the back, and attacked him with bricks. He ended up blinded in one eye, with severe injuries to his tongue and throat, 50 percent burns over his body, and fractures to his face. He is on life support in Broomfield Hospital, Chelmsford. His condition is described as critical but stable.

One eyewitness recalled: "I saw four men lashing out and kicking him on the ground. I shouted and they ran off, then one went back and started on him again. The poor man got up and ran straight into a tree, then staggered back to his house, tugging at his burning clothes and banging on doors shouting for water." Kay Dice, 52, another witness, added: "He was screaming and screaming, but he spoke little English and some people thought he may have just had too much to drink. I thought he had a huge cross on his back, but it was where his skin had peeled away."

The police arrested seven young men. Five are free on bail and two, ages 19 and 25, have appeared in court, charged with attempted murder. (July 23, 2009)

Homosexuals punished or killed: A topic conspicuously missing here, so far, is the treatment of Muslim homosexual men in the West. To give some idea of the problem, here are some extracts from a study out today from Human Rights Watch, "'They Want Us Exterminated': Murder, Torture, Sexual Orientation and Gender in Iraq," about the same issue in Iraq: In addition to women, men

> also bear the "honor" of their families and tribes. Human Rights Watch heard testimonies from Iraqi men who faced violence or murder because they were not "manly" enough, incurring shame on the whole extended household. These stories suggest the importance of treating "honor" as an issue, and an incitement to rights violations, that cuts across genders.

Punishments for not being "man" enough start when young.

> "Since I was 12, my father and my brothers beat and insulted me for my feminine appearance and behavior," Tayyib, 24, from Baghdad, told us. "My father beat me all the time, and he also burned my hands and arms with heated metal. My brothers would beat me up whenever they saw me playing with girls, for example. My mother tried to protect me, but she couldn't do anything to stop it."

The study goes on to give several other accounts along these lines. (August 17, 2009)

Attempt at male honor killing goes awry, innocent couple killed: A jury in the Preston Crown Court in Lancashire, England, is hearing a case involving an attempted honor killing of a male lover:

Hafija Gorji was having marital troubles with her husband. Then, as Brian Cummings QC, prosecuting, recounts: "In April of last year she met Mo Ibrahim at a wedding, found him attractive and sent text messages. It soon progressed to a sexual relationship between them. In September her husband found out about the affair and assaulted her. She went to the police scared that her husband would go to Mo's house and cause a disturbance." Detectives then questioned Mo Ibrahim, who confirmed the affair and related having received a phone call from Hafija's husband, who demanded that he swear on the Koran before her family that there was nothing between them.

Less than a month later, to punish Mo Ibrahim on behalf of the family for his sexual relationship with Hafija, her brother Hisamuddin Ibrahim, 21 (no relation) ordered a fire-bombing. According to the prosecution, Hisamuddin Ibrahim, who lives in London, got three young men—Habib Iqbal, Mohammed Miah, and Sadek Miah (no relation), to drive from London to Blackburn to carry out the attack on Mo in the early hours of October 21, 2009, at his residence, 135 London Road. But, armed with a can of petrol, the trio confused the house and instead attacked 175 London Road, killing Abdullah Mohammed, 41, and his wife, Aysha Mohammed, 39.

Sadek Miah has pleaded guilty to manslaughter; his co-defendants have all pleaded not guilty. The trial continues. (July 3, 2010)

| *"The death-toll exacted by the blood feud has historically been heavy for Balkans men."*

Blood Feuds Are Gendercide Against Men in the Balkans

Adam Jones

Adam Jones is a political scientist at the University of British Columbia Okanagan and executive director of Gendercide Watch. In the following viewpoint, he discusses the blood feud in the Balkans, which he suggests is a counterpart to female honor killings. In blood feuds, the killing of one family member results in retaliation by the victim's family against any male member of the killer's family. The result, Jones says, is an escalating string of murders of men in the name of honor. Killing women is seen as dishonorable, and so women are able to pursue their usual business, while men hide in their homes for fear of being murdered.

As you read, consider the following questions:

1. What is the Kanun of Lek Dukagjin, and how does it affect blood feuds, as described by the author?

2. According to Jones, how did the blood feud give rise to the institution of the "sworn virgin"?

3. What are the origins of the current blood-feud crisis in Albania, in the author's opinion?

The institution of the "blood feud" is the little-known but highly-destructive male counterpart to "honour" killings of women. Every year, at least a thousand men and boys die in blood-feud killings in Albania alone; the lives of tens of thousands more are spent in isolation and perpetual fear. Women and girls are virtually never targeted.

Honor in the Balkans

The Balkans [a peninsula between Italy and Turkey], along with the Caucasus region [between the Black and Caspian Seas], Sicily, and Corsica [islands off Italy], are the areas where the "blood feud" still holds greatest sway today. (In the past, the institution was also prominent in Scotland—and in the U.S. region of Appalachia, as with the famous feud between the Hatfields and McCoys.)

The institution of the blood feud is most virulent in the *malësi* (mountain regions) of northern Albania, spilling over into the territory that is today the Yugoslav province of Kosovo. The institution has its roots in the *Kanun* (canon) of Lek Dukagjin, a legal code compiled in the fifteenth century that enshrined "many customary practices which went back much further into the past," according to Noel Malcolm. Malcolm writes that

> The importance of the *Kanun* to the ordinary life of the Albanians of Kosovo and the Malësi can hardly be exaggerated.... One leading scholar has summed up the basic principles of the *Kanun* as follows. The foundation of it all is the principle of personal honour. Next comes the equality of persons. From these flows a third principle, the freedom of each to act in accordance with his own honour, within the limits of the law, without being subject to

another's command. And the fourth principle is the word of honour, the *besë* ... which creates a situation of inviolable trust. Gjeçov's version of the Kanun ["the fullest and most authoritative text"] decrees: "An offence to honour is not paid for with property, but by spilling of blood or a magnanimous pardon." And it specifies the ways of dishonouring a man, of which the most important are calling him a liar in front of other men; insulting his wife; taking his weapons; or violating his hospitality. . . . This was very much a man's world. . . . Women had their honour, but it existed through, and was defended by, men. (Malcolm, *Kosovo: A Short History*, pp. 18–19.)

The blood feud was the result of perceived violations of this code of "honour." It "is one of the most archaic features of northern Albanian society," notes Malcolm. ". . .What lies at the heart of the blood-feud is a concept alien to the modern mind, and more easily learned about from the plays of [ancient Greek writer] Aeschylus than from the works of modern sociologists: the aim is not punishment of a murderer, but satisfaction of the blood of the person murdered—or, initially, satisfaction of one's own honour when it has been polluted. If retribution were the real aim, then only those personally responsible for the original crime or insult would be potential targets; but instead, honour is cleansed by killing any male member of the family of the original offender, and the spilt blood of that victim then cries out to its own family for purification." The blood feud granted blanket exemption to females, the killing of whom was seen as a profound violation of a *man's* personal honour. "The strongest taboo of all concerned the murder of women, and any woman could walk through raging gunfire in the knowledge that she would never be shot at." (Malcolm, *Kosovo: A Short History*, pp. 19–20.)

Men as Targets

In his study of the blood-feud in the Yugoslav province of Montenegro, Christopher Boehm gives a vivid picture of the surreal lengths to which this gender-selectivity is carried:

In the old days, women were free to come and go as they chose under feuding conditions, since taking their blood did nothing to help the blood score and also counted as a dishonor, morally speaking. Thus, their normal daily activities could continue. But men were sorely pressed when it came to doing any work other than herding, which allowed them to stay under cover with a rifle ready at all times. In 1965 [at the time of field research] it was for this reason that women still did so much of the heavier work in the fields, so I was told by the slightly apologetic Montenegrin "male chauvinists," who viewed this as a once-necessary custom formed in an earlier era. . . . Whatever might happen to the men during a feud, the women were always free to keep the household economy going because the rules of feuding were taken so seriously by the opposing party.

With respect to the sanctity of women, it was even possible for them to enter directly into combat during the first stage of a feud, when the killer's clan shut itself in and the victim's clan attacked the fortified stone farmhouse, which had loopholes [for firing rifles] everywhere. With no fear of being harmed, women could carry straw and firebrands up to the house to try to burn it. Also, women of a besieged house could go outside at night carrying torches, to light up the enemy so that their own men could shoot at them. This exemplifies the strength of these particular rules: to shoot a woman was a source of shame (*sramota*) for the entire clan. (Boehm, *Blood Revenge: The Anthropology of Feuding in Montenegro and Other Tribal Societies*, pp. 111–12.)

The death-toll exacted by the blood feud has historically been heavy for Balkans men. "At the end of the Ottoman period [in the early twentieth century] it was estimated that 19 percent of all adult male deaths in the Malësi were blood-feud murders, and that in an area of Western Kosovo with 50,000 inhabitants, 600 died in these feuds every year." (Malcolm, *Kosovo: A Short History*, p. 20.) In Albania, the feuds gave rise to another enduring institution: the "sworn virgin," women who "cut their hair short, wear trousers and drink fiery local brandy with the men." According to Julius Strauss, "The tradition of the sworn virgins was born of necessity in this barren land racked by war, blood feuds and intense poverty. In times past when the male line of a family was wiped out, such a virgin was entitled to take over as the head of the family." (Strauss, "The Virgins Who Live Like Men," *The Daily Telegraph* [London], February 6, 1997.)

The Return of the Blood Feud

Blood feuds generally declined in the Balkans after the Second World War, as the authoritarian rulers of Albania (Enver Hoxha) and Yugoslavia (Josip Broz Tito) clamped down on practices that were seen as a legacy of the feudal past. In Albania, however, the blood feud has returned with—one might say—a vengeance. It has also spread from the traditional heartland of the Malësi to Tirana, the capital, and to the south of the country.

The origins of the current blood-feud crisis in Albania date to the collapse of the communist regime in 1991, and the weakness of the quasi-democratic government that replaced it. From 1992 to 1996, "press reports in Tirana" spoke of "more than 5,000 murders linked to vendettas in the past four years." (Branko Jolis, "Honour Killing Makes a Comeback," *The Guardian* [Manchester, UK], August 14, 1996.) It is worth noting that this rate of approximately 1,250 men killed in blood feuds annually is slightly greater than the number of known "honour" killings of women in Pakistan—in a country with about 1/35th the population. Estimates of fatalities are made difficult by the fact that many blood-feud murders go unreported. As one Albanian clan leader told *The New York Times*, "People don't want to report killings to the police because then the accused would be protected by the state in prison instead of being available to kill." (Jane Perlez, "Blood Feuds Draining a Fierce Corner of Albania," *The New York Times*, April 15, 1998.)

In March 1997, the post-communist regime was rocked by "the collapse of enormous, government-endorsed pyramid investment schemes. The public looted army weapons depots as furious investors clashed with security forces. Roughly 1 million firearms are said to be in circulation in a Balkan nation of only 3.2 million." (Michael J. Jordan, "In Albania, A Return to 'Eye for Eye,'" *The Christian Science Monitor*, August 7, 1997.) Between 1,600 and 5,000 Albanians died in the ensuing six months, and "revenge killings skyrocketed." (Perlez, "Blood Feuds.") In 1998, Gjin Mekshi, a leader of the Committee of Blood Reconciliation in the town of Shkoder, stated that "In some families there are no men left," although "So far no women have been killed." (Owen Bowcott, "Thousands of Albanian Children in Hiding to Escape Blood Feuds," *The Guardian* [Manchester, UK], September 30, 1998.)

No Men Left

In addition to the thousands killed, tens of thousands of men live in fear and seclusion as a result of the blood feuds. Mihaela Rodina cites estimates by Albanian non-governmental organizations that "the men of some 25,000 families in northern Albania live thus, never going out of the house for fear of being victims of . . . feuding. The women, who are unaffected by the *kanun*, are left alone to provide for the family's needs." (Rodina, "Blood Code Rules in Northern Albania," Agence France-Presse dispatch, June 30, 1999.) In 1997, *The Christian Science Monitor* interviewed one man in Shkoder who "ha[d] been homebound for six years. . . . The man says he dreams of escaping with a visa to America. 'This is actually worse than prison,' he says, standing in his fenced-in garden. 'At least in prison I'd know that one day I could get out.'" Even school-age boys must remain cloistered: "up to 6,000 children [were] said to be hiding" in 1998. (Bowcott, "Thousands of Albanian Children.")

An Albanian Blood Feud

On the afternoon of August 3, 1998, forty-three-year-old Shtjefen Lamthi was walking through one of the main streets in Shkoder, Albania. As he passed a small tobacco kiosk, a man in his mid-thirties stepped into Lamthi's path, brought up a Kalashnikov assault rifle, and shot him. As Lamthi fell, the murderer shot him twenty-one more times, emptying the rifle's ammo clip. The assailant walked away, and none of the two hundred people who witnessed the murder came forward to identify him. As war correspondent Scott Anderson reported in a *New York Times Magazine* article in 1999, this was a classic example of an honor killing based on the Albanian notion of *kanun*. The *kanun* is a book of rules and oaths that, if you live in the Albanian outback, require you to give your complete allegiance to your family and community. Blood vengeance by murder can become a sacred duty to defend the honor of your family. Shtjefen Lamthi's murder, by Leka Rrushkadoli, was such a murder, avenging a death occurring thirteen years earlier.

At its core, the *kanun* is about defending honor, since a man who has been dishonored is considered dead. Small offenses and dishonors can be settled through more peaceful means, while greater offenses require vengeance killings. Under the *kanun*, murder is the ultimate dishonor to a family. The family lives in disgrace until it can obtain revenge by killing the killer. Of course, once this is done, the killer's family is in disgrace, and the cycle must repeat itself. Occasionally, these conflicts are mediated to peace, but not very often.

Douglas E. Noll, Elusive Peace: How Modern Diplomatic Strategies Could Better Resolve World Conflicts, *2011.*

The resurgence of the blood feud has led Gjin Mekshi and others to join forces in an attempt to reconcile feuding families. "The Committee of Blood Reconciliation has 3,000 members in Albania and is pressing the government to accept its arbitrations as part of the legal process. 'I have a good reputation and my father was a man of good reputation, too,' says Mr. Mekshi. 'I am approached to arrange truces by those who are in hiding and dare not go out during the day. When we agree [to] a deal, we sanctify the arrangement with a procession led by the local priest." (Bowcott, "Thousands of Albanian Children.") Albanian Radio reported in August 2000 that "Seven hundred and fifty-six blood feuds have been reconciled, allowing the people involved to put an end to self-confinement at home." (BBC Worldwide Monitoring, August 10, 2000.) In neighbouring Kosovo, a similar campaign was mounted in the 1990s by Anton Çetta. (Malcolm, *Kosovo: A Short History*, p. 20.) Nonetheless, according to Deutsche Presse-Agentur, the success of such campaigns has been "only limited." ("Albanian Blood Feuds Affect 210,000," Deutsche Presse-Agentur, March 11, 2000.) "The feuds have very deep roots," said Perlat Ramgaj, mayor of the town of Koplik. "They're ingrained on our souls, and in this period of transition people feel free to do just about anything." (Quoted in Helena Smith, "Lost Land Where Vengeance Is Written in Blood," *The Guardian*, February 12, 1995.)

I | *"Rape has become more and more tactical and strategic during wartime."*

Women Are Targeted for Violence in War

Sandra I. Cheldelin

Sandra I. Cheldelin is a Professor of Conflict Resolution at George Mason University in Virginia. In the following viewpoint she argues that women are targeted for rape and sexual violence in war. She contends that rape is used as a weapon of terror and that women are also seen as "war booty," and raped as a "reward" by enemy soldiers. She discusses mass rapes in Germany by Russian soldiers after World War II, Japanese rapes of Chinese women in World War II, and other, more recent incidents and concludes that sexual violence against women in wartime is endemic to genocidal violence.

As you read, consider the following questions:

1. What difficulty did Susan Brownmiller have in making stories of wartime rape public, according to the author?

2. How were American occupation troops during World War II provided with "war booty" according to Cheldelin?

© Sandra I. Cheldelin, 2011, *Women Waging War and Peace: International Perspective on Women's Roles in Conflict and Post Conflict Resolution*, Bloomsbury Publishing Inc.

3. According to the author, how many Chinese were raped and killed during the Japanese occupation of Nanjing?

Sexual violence during wartime is well documented. The primary story that emerges is that women are victims of the most unimaginable and inhumane behavior. This type of gendered wartime violence is nothing new. Rape and torture have been integral parts of wars from the beginning. As Swiss and Giller (1993) note, there are written records of wartime rape from ancient Greece. They go on to describe that "the induction of Helen of Troy and the rape of the Sabine women are archetypal in Western culture, so much so that their human tragedy is obscured". Whether the victors take conquered women home as sexual slaves, sexually assault them as punishment for their opponents' resistance, use them to satisfy their sexual desires, or hold them hostage until impregnation, rape has and continues to threaten women and girls in every conflict across the globe throughout the millennia. The many cases of atrocities offer insights into the trauma and challenges faced by victims and members of their families and communities.

Stories of Rape

As rape has become more and more tactical and strategic during wartime, the horrors of such torture lead to prolonged psychological damage or death and can no longer be dismissed. In this [viewpoint] we witness the underbelly of all wars and are challenged as a moral imperative to intervene. . . .

Several personal accounts set the context. The first is presented by Nat Hentoff in the *Village Voice* (February 2001) in response to a *New York Times* editorial on the government of Sudan's terrorism against black Christians and animists in the southern part of the country. The *Times* focused on the national Muslim military regime that had targeted black Africans and, as a result, more than four million southern Sudanese were displaced—the most displaced in the world. Clearly this was an atrocity but so, too, was what was known to the editor but not reported: the extraordinary personal horrors experienced by women like then 20-year-old Aluel Mangong Deng. In her own words, she tells of her abduction story in southern Sudan [reported by Hentoff]:

> I was enslaved five years ago [1996] during a raid on my village, Agok. I tried to run away from the soldiers, but they caught me and threw me to the ground. I struggled to get away, so they held down my hands and feet and cut my throat and chest with a knife. As I grew faint, one of them named Mohammed raped me then and there. That night, I was again raped by different men. They came one after another. This also happened to other women, and even to young girls. It took about 30 days before we reached Poulla, north of Babanusa. This kind of rape happened just about every day along the way.

When Deng desperately tried to escape from her captors she was brutally gang-raped while simultaneously having her throat slit. As she endured this violence, she was told of her inferiority based on her ethnicity. Spending years as a slave—where she also suffered repeated gang rapes—Deng finally escaped and was discovered in a displaced persons camp in southern Sudan. Why was this left out of the *New York Times* account of Sudan's terrorism? Are the horrors of women such as Deng not newsworthy?

A second story is told by Jasmine Tesanovic about a 19-year-old woman who lived with her family in Bosnia. As the war began her brothers fought for the Serbs while she hid in basements in the army-occupied part of her country. One day her luck ran out, and she was found and raped by soldiers. When it was discovered that she was pregnant, her father banned her from their home but later stated that he would allow her to return if she had a boy. Again a misfortune; the baby was a girl. Desperate, she gave her baby for adoption and went home. Soon, though, she was overwhelmed with guilt, returned to her village to find her child, reclaimed her, and relocated to another town. Not long after, a friend found her standing on the ledge of a window. The friend successfully coaxed her down, and in the ensuing conversation she explained that when she looked at her baby's face—whom she loved more than anyone—she saw her rapist's face—whom she despised more than anyone. Her options seemed limited to either killing herself or killing her baby.

Tesanovic's story was not uncommon in 2003 and again in 2005 when I interviewed women of the Association of Concentration Camp Torture Survivors of Canton Sarajevo, though at that point their situations were slightly more complicated. The children that resulted from their rapes were now preadolescents. Many of the women and their children were not welcome in their former communities, banned from their families, medically impaired, dealing with long-term psychological illnesses and depression, and economically desperate.

Another account of wartime rape comes from the Congo. Chris McGreal [of the Manchester (UK) *Guardian*] tells the poignant story of a then-23-year-old woman from Walikali, a territory within the Congolese province in the eastern regions of the Democratic Republic of the Congo (DRC), who was among the thousands attacked in her country. She travelled 90 miles to a hospital for surgery in Goma after the Rwandan Hutu militia gang-raped her. In her words:

> Where I lived they were in the forest . . . we had to go there to find food. There were four of us and we were stopped by seven Interahamwe. [We] tried to run away. One was shot dead. The other got a bullet in the leg. They still raped her. I fainted because there were seven of them. I really got damaged. I couldn't hold in my urine. I heard these people came back and killed my father.

Also a victim of the Hutu militia was a 54-year-old woman from Kindu, the capital of Maniema province in the DRC, who was repeatedly raped by a group of Mai Mai, an ethnic militia in her area. She states:

They came in the morning and raped me, two of them. That didn't disturb me so much after what happened later. In the afternoon five men came into the house. They told my husband to put three kinds of money on the table: dollars, shillings, francs. But we didn't have any of that kind of money. We are poor. We don't even know what dollars look like. So they shot him. My children were screaming and so they shot them. After that they raped me, all of them.

McGreal reports that as the woman lay bleeding the attackers thrust the barrels of their guns into her vagina. The Doctors on Call Service (DOCS) hospital in Goma have treated thousands of rape victims such as the woman from Kindu. One in four requires surgery, and more than one-third are under 18.

Rape and War

[Feminist author Susan] Brownmiller provides insight as to how difficult it is to make the war/rape story public in her introductory paragraphs on the *Women of 1971* website documenting the rape in Bangladesh. In 1971, Brownmiller read in the *New York Post* that the government of Bangladesh was declaring all of the women raped by Pakistani military "heroines" of the war for seeking independence. The concluding sentence read, "In the traditional Bengali village society, where women lead cloistered lives, rape victims often are ostracized." This story launched her research. She asked a friend who worked on the foreign desk of the *New York Times* about a story on the "Rape of Bengali Women" and reports that he merely laughed: "I don't think so. It doesn't sound like a *Times* story." Similarly, a friend at *Newsweek* was "skeptical." She states, "I got the distinct impression that both men, good journalists, thought I was barking up an odd tree. NBC's Liz Trotta was one of the few American reporters to investigate the Bangladesh rape story at this time. She filed a TV report for the weekend news." Is this just weekend news? Was Hentoff right—that rape is not *New York Times* (or *Newsweek*) worthy?

Individual stories of horrific crimes demand an empathic response, but when we consider the collective stories—all of the women raped and tortured in all of the wars—it is clear that rape is a gendered crime and requires comprehensive and persistent interventions. The data that follow, provided by the United Nations Office for the Coordination of Humanitarian Affairs (OCHA), seem almost unimaginable. While the number raped in Vietnam is unknown, in the 1980s in South Africa, 25,000 women were raped. During the Bosnia-Herzegovina war, 1992–1993, there were 20,000 to 70,000 raped. In 1994, 250,000 women were raped in Rwanda, which resulted in 2,500 to 10,000 pregnancies. In just the first six months of 2006, more than 12,000 rapes of women and girls occurred in eastern Congo. It will be years before a complete account of the numbers will be available as rape continues there.

Rape has no boundaries of age. As [Jan] Goodwin reports [in a 2004 *Nation* article], Maria, age 70, was victim to the Hutu militia that led Rwanda's 1994 genocide and who are now part of the 140,000 rebels in the DRC. They came to Maria's home and in her words:

> They grabbed me, tied my legs apart like a goat before slaughter, then raped me, one after the other. Then they stuck sticks inside me until I think. . . . War came. I just saw smoke and fire. Then my life and my health were taken away.

Maria's entire family—five sons, three daughters, and her husband—were murdered. "She was left with a massive fistula [an abnormal connection or passage between organs] where her bladder was torn, causing permanent incontinence. She hid in the Bush for three years out of fear that the rebels might return, and out of shame over her constantly soiled clothes".

A Danger to All

The greatest threat to civilian women during conflict is rape and sexual violence by armed, uniformed, state and nonstate forces and civilians. That means that in the 35 countries currently in conflict, being a civilian woman in these countries will likely result in being violated. It is and has been commonplace for centuries for rape and sexual violence against women to go unchallenged. Only in the past quarter century, when human rights organizations began to document testimony from women, have the doors opened to provide a voice for these victims. Prior to documentation, though, no one will ever know the extent of damage women and girls experienced from assaults.

Unfortunately even now, with laws in place to convict perpetrators, women must testify, sign indictments, and deal with the family and community fallout. "If they admit rape, women cannot protect their children from rape, from suffering social stigmas" ([according to feminist writer Jasmina] Tesanovic). So there remains the shame, the humiliation, and ultimately silence for the majority of women victims. Anneke Van Woudenberg, a Congo specialist for Human Rights Watch (HRW), tells of a 30-year-old in North Kivu who was brutalized to make sure she would not identify or testify against her attackers:

> [She] had her lips and ears cut off and eyes gouged out after she was raped. . . . Now, we are seeing more and more such cases . . . as the rebels constantly seek new ways to terrorize, their barbarity becomes more frenzied. . . . Gang-raped victims [have] their labia [genital area] pierced and then padlocked. 'They usually die of massive infection,' I was told" [according to Goodwin].

A medical team of researchers reported in the *Journal of American Medical Association (JAMA)* their survey results on the prevalence of rape and sexual violence in eastern Congo and their assessment of basic health care needs and available access. From their door-to-door interviews of more than 1,000 villagers in north and south Kivu and Ituri, they confirmed widespread incidence of rape: Nearly 40 percent of women (and 23 percent of men) had suffered sexual assault, and sexual violence victims had mental health disorders at twice the population rate.

A controversial finding, too, was the number of women reported as perpetrators of sexual assault—41 percent of the assaulted women and 10 percent of the men reported they were victim to women. Caution was advised from the head of the US-based NGO [nongovernmental organization] International Rescue Committee (IRC) in the DRC, Ciáran Donnelly. He confirmed the findings of . . . high level of sexual violence and its impact but suggests further investigation needs to be conducted on the gender-based perpetrator data. It is not clear, for example, "whether women kidnapped by armed groups [were] forced to perform sexual acts on others [and therefore became] the perpetrators of conflict-related sexual violence". Clearly the rape/war problem is complicated when women, too, resort to rape and violence, regardless of whether or not they are women under duress. . . .

War Booty

A longstanding excuse for the persistence of rape during and after war is the "war booty" thesis wherein the rape of "enemy women" is accepted as fair game or as a just reward for victory. . . .

The "war booty" thesis is remarkably chronicled in *A Woman in Berlin: Eight Weeks in the Conquered City* written by a female German journalist who details two months surrounding the arrival of Soviet troops at the end of [World War II]. After the first time that Soviet soldiers raped her— the first of many men to rape her many times—she writes:

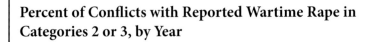

Percent of Conflicts with Reported Wartime Rape in Categories 2 or 3, by Year

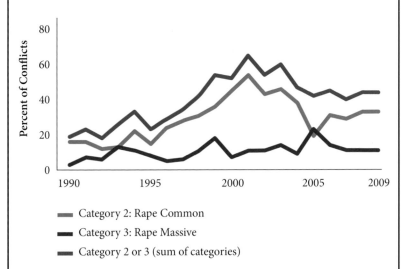

- Category 2: Rape Common
- Category 3: Rape Massive
- Category 2 or 3 (sum of categories)

TAKEN FROM: Amelia Hoover Green, Dara Kay Cohen, Elisabeth Jeanwood, "Is Wartime Rape Declining on a Global Scale? We Don't Know—And It Doesn't Matter," *Political Violence at a Glance*, November 1, 2012. http://politicalviolenceataglance.org

One of them grabs my wrists and jerks me along the corridor. Then the other is pulling as well, his hands on my throat, so I can no longer scream. I no longer want to scream, for fear of being strangled. They're both tearing away at me; instantly I'm on the floor. . . . I end up with my head on the bottom step of the basement stairs. I can feel the damp coolness of the floor tiles. The door above is ajar and lets in a little light. One man stands there keeping watch, while the other tears my underclothes, forcing his way . . . [I] grope around the floor with my left hand until I find my key ring. I hold it tight. I use my right hand to defend myself. It's no use. He's simply torn off my garter, ripping it in two. When I struggle to come up, the second one throws himself on me as well, forcing me back on the ground with his fists and knees. Now the other keeps lookout, whispering, "Hurry up, hurry."

Following the fall of the Nazi regime in 1945, it is estimated that more than 100,000 German women were raped in Berlin by their Russian conquerors. For the average Russian soldier, the conquest of Berlin meant an entitlement to the German women of the city after a long and difficult war. The mass rapes in Berlin were not used as a strategy of war; rather they symbolized revenge, sexual gratification, and just reward. [An] anonymous [woman]'s diary supports this assertion. She overhears a conversation between Russian soldiers about "Stalin's decree" that seems to suggest that [Soviet leader Joseph] Stalin had "declared that 'this kind of thing' [rape] is not to happen". Stalin may not have endorsed the mass rape, but neither did he act to stop it.

The rapes usually occurred at night after the Russian soldiers had consumed a great deal of alcohol; the alcohol presumably helped to lower inhibitions against sexual violence. The German men were by and large unable to protect their women, and the author writes of the men's misery and powerlessness. "The weaker sex. Deep down we women are experiencing a kind of collective disappointment". [She] also tacitly writes about the shameful experience of the German men: "I think our men must feel even dirtier than we do, sullied as we women are". It was expected that the German women of Berlin would be forced to acquiesce to the Russian soldiers, and by doing so, they were the ones who were able to protect their men against the wrath of the Russian soldiers. . . .

The notion of war booty was evident during World War II when the Japanese armed forces had access to the hundreds of thousands of Koreans and Chinese women kidnapped and enslaved as "comfort women." These women were forced to provide sexual services to the Japanese, and following the war, the Japanese set up sexual service stations for American GIs "with the tacit approval from the US occupation authorities who had full knowledge that women were being coerced into prostitution" [according to *Washington Post* writer Eric Talmadge].

A day before the Japanese began their negotiation for the country's surrender and occupation—September 19, 1945—the Ibaraki police were told to set up sexual comfort stations for the occupation troops. They converted a police officer dormitory into a brothel, "stocking" it with 20 women. The next day it was operating. For the cost of one dollar—the price of a half pack of cigarettes—paid up front, GIs received a ticket and a condom. When the first brothel opened, a line of more than 500 occupying GIs immediately formed. Each woman served 15 to 60 clients per day. Seven months later, General [Douglas] MacArthur declared all places of prostitution off limits—his decision likely was informed by medical necessity as nearly a quarter of the 35,000 troops had contracted sexually transmitted diseases.

Gendered War

Though the war booty thesis is documented and persistent over the centuries, the latter part of the twentieth century, especially, is witness to an even more horrifying and sinister use of war rape. It is mass rape as a deliberate, state-sanctioned strategy of war to exterminate a race of people, also known as genocide. Mary Anne Warren [in her 1985 book *Gendercide*] makes a further distinction, the deliberate extermination of a particular sex (or gender), known as gendercide. Illustrations of female infanticide, maternal mortality, and the witch-hunts in early modern Europe (and the United States) are explored by Warren. *Gendercide Watch* summarizes 22 current and historical gendercide cases including atrocities in Armenia (1915–1917), the Jewish Holocaust (1933–1945), Nanjing (1937–1938), the many Stalin's Purges, Bangladesh (1971), the Kashmir/Punjab/Delhi massacre (1984), Bosnia-Herzegovina (1992–1995), Rwanda (1994), Srebrenica [Bosnia] (1995), Kosovo (1998–1999), East Timor (1999), and Colombia (since 1948). The state-sanctioned gender-selective mass killings over the years have overwhelmingly targeted "battle-age" men, and Gendercide Watch is concerned that ignoring the massive male killings "is one of the great taboos of the contemporary age, and must be ignored no longer". Their collective case analyses offer data about the ways in which men and women are targeted; rape continues to be the dominant tool against women. . . .

Nanjing Massacre

During the Japanese invasion of Nanjing, China, in 1937, 20,000 to 80,000 women were raped by the Imperial Japanese Army; 300,000 men, women, and children were killed. The Nanjing Massacre, also known as the Rape of Nanking (Nanjing), is a case of gendercide against both women and men. While the invading Japanese gang-raped women—then killed them or left them tortured and traumatized—they rounded up 250,000 Chinese civilian men as prisoners of war and [according to Gendercide Watch] "murdered them *en masse*, used for bayonet practice, or burned and buried [them] alive." [In her 1998 book *The Rape of Nanking* Iris] Chang writes that "surviving Japanese veterans claim that the army had officially outlawed the rape of enemy women, but the military policy forbidding rape only encouraged soldiers to kill their victims afterwards". The callous nature of the rape and killings is reflected in a soldier's recollection that

> It would be all right if we only raped them. I shouldn't say all right. But we always stabbed and killed them. Because dead bodies don't talk. . . . Perhaps when we were raping her, we looked at her as a woman, but when we killed her, we just thought of her as something like a pig.

Other Japanese soldiers report that they [according to James Yin and Shi Young's 1996 book *The Rape of Nanking*] "were hungry for women" and were told to use bayonets or rifles to kill the women after they were raped so that no one would be able to trace the killers.

Many who witnessed the massacre have captured its gruesome qualities. Li Ke-hen is quoted in Yin and Young:

> There are so many bodies on the street, victims of group rape and murder. They were all stripped naked, their breasts cut off, leaving a terrible dark brown hole; some of them were bayoneted in the abdomen, with their intestines spilling out alongside them; some had a roll of paper or a piece of wood stuffed in their vaginas.

Another account, from the diary of a German Nazi businessman, is quoted in Chang:

> Groups of 3 to 10 marauding soldiers would begin by traveling through the city and robbing whatever there was to steal. They would continue by raping the women and girls and killing anything and anyone that offered any resistance, attempted to run away from them or simply happened to be in the wrong place at the wrong time. There were girls under the age of 8 and women over the age of 70 who were raped and then, in the most brutal way possible, knocked down and beat up.

The war memorial of the Nanjing Massacre introduces visitors at its entrance to dramatic and moving larger-than-life sculptures depicting the horror and sorrow of this six-week catastrophe. The first has a man dragging his wife, and the caption on the sculpture of *The Helpless Struggle of a Dying Intellectual* reads: "My dear poor wife! The devil raped you, killed you. . . . I'm right after you!" The second sculpture shows an old man leading two children away and looking toward the sky: "The devils have sent the bombers again. . . . The poor orphans, Frightened by the vicious laughter of the brutal devils, Terrified by the corps[es] piling up in the alley, Have lapsed into numbness." There is also a statue of an elder son guiding his mother: "My dear mother in the eighties,

Hurry up! Run away from the bloody hands." One sculpture of a woman partially clothed and in despair bears these words: "Never will a holy soul bear the humiliation of the devils! Only to die! Only to die! Only death can wash the filth away!" Finally, a sorrowful child is sitting looking at his dead mother: "Frigidity and horror have frozen this crying baby! Poor thing. Not knowing mum has been killed, Blood, milk and tears, Have frozen, never melting."

On a wall inside the memorial are captions of verdicts from the International Military Tribunal of the Far East and the Nanjing Military Tribunal for the Trial of War Criminals. One poignant statement reads: "After the seizure of the city the Japanese army went raping everywhere to satisfy their sexual lust. . . . On December 16–17, Chinese women raped by Japanese soldiers exceeded one thousand. The ways they performed such atrocities are appalling and cruel, unprecedented in the world history. . . . Every woman left in Nanjing found themselves jeopardized."

"With the exception of sexual violence and intimate partner violence, males are more likely than females to be the victims of violence."

Men Are Disproportionally Targeted for Violence and Gendercide

David Benatar

David Benatar is a professor of philosophy at the University of Cape Town in South Africa. In the following viewpoint, he argues that men are statistically and historically more at risk of violence and murder than are women. He says that women are more likely to be victims of sexual violence, and comparably likely to be victims of intimate partner violence. For other kinds of violence, including assaults, murders, and genocidal violence, he says that men are disproportionately targeted and are disproportionately victimized.

As you read, consider the following questions:

1. According to Benatar, what do studies show about the incidence and effect of spousal violence against men and women?

2. Who does Benatar say behave more aggressively against men than against women?

3. In South Africa under apartheid, how many more men than women died, according to the Truth and Reconciliation Commission?

With two exceptions, men are much more likely than women to be the targets of aggression and violence.

The first exception is sexual assault. Although . . . the incidence of sexual assault of males is significantly underestimated and taken insufficiently seriously, it is the case that women are more frequently the victims of sexual assault.

The second exception is one kind of domestic violence, but this is exceptional in an unusual way. In its spousal or "intimate partner" form, the phrase "domestic violence" is routinely understood to refer to the violence husbands or boyfriends inflict on wives or girlfriends. The general perception is that spousal violence is almost exclusively the violent treatment of women by their husbands, boyfriends or other male partners. However, this perception is mistaken. Many studies have shown that wives use violence against their husbands at least as much as husbands use violence against their wives. Given how unexpected such findings are to many people, at least one well-known author (who shared the prevailing prejudices prior to his quantitative research) examined the data in multiple ways in order to determine whether these could be reconciled with common views. On almost every score, women were as violent as men. It was found that half the violence is mutual, and in the remaining half there were an equal number of female and male aggressors. When a distinction was drawn between "normal violence" (pushing, shoving, slapping and throwing things) and "severe violence" (kicking, biting, punching, hitting with an object, "beating up" and attacking the spouse with a knife or gun), the rate of mutual violence dropped to a third, the rate of violence by only the husband remained the same but the rate of violence by only the wife *increased*. Wives have been shown to initiate violence as often as husbands do. At least some studies have suggested that there is a *higher* rate of wives assaulting husbands than husbands assaulting wives, and most studies of dating violence show higher rates of female-inflicted violence. It is thus not the case, as some have suggested, that female violence against intimate partners is usually in self-defense.

Research findings on the *effects* of spousal violence are mixed. Some have found that husbands inflict more damage on wives than wives do on husbands. It has been suggested that this is because husbands are generally bigger and stronger than their wives. However, other studies have found that wives inflict more damage on husbands. If weapons are used, the smaller size of women would make no difference to their capacity to cause injury. Yet other studies have found no difference in the severity of injury caused by male and female partners.

Thus spousal violence is an exception to the trend that men are at *greater* risk of being the victims of violence, not because men are at *lesser* risk but because they are at *comparable* risk. However, the mistaken perception that wives do not batter husbands itself causes further disadvantage to males. Abused men are taken less seriously than abused women when they complain of abuse or seek help. There are also fewer resources to aid abused men.

Violence, Murder, Genocide

With the exception of sexual violence and intimate partner violence, males are more likely than females to be the victims of violence. Both men and women have been shown, in a majority of experimental studies, to behave more aggressively against men than toward women. Outside the laboratory, men are also more often the victims of violence. This is true in a variety of contexts. Consider first violent crime. Data from the

USA, for example, shows that nearly double the number of men as women are the victims of aggravated assault and more than three times more men than women are murdered. Statistics from England and Wales show a similar phenomenon there. During the 2008–2009 year, men "were twice as likely as women to have been victims of violence." Young men, aged 16 to 24 were particularly at risk. Thirteen percent of them had been the victims of violent crime, compared with 3% of all adults.

In cases of conflict, men, even when they are not combatants, suffer more violence. For example, the overwhelming majority of deaths during the Belgian "rubber terror" in the Congo were males. Although there is apparently no direct evidence of the numbers killed, the subsequent significant demographic imbalance between the number of adult males and females in the population at the end of this period reveals that it was primarily male lives that were taken.

Men were also the majority of victims of the Stalinist purges. Examining data from the Soviet census of January 1959, Robert Conquest concluded that although the casualties of war explain some of the sex imbalance in the population, the more significant imbalances were in older age cohorts that were less affected by combat losses in the Second World War and more affected by the purges. Thus, in the 55–59 age group, only 33% of the population was male. In the adjacent age cohorts, the proportions are very similar. About 38% of 40- to 54-year-olds were male, and nearly 35% of 60- to 69-year-olds were male.

In South Africa, the Truth and Reconciliation Commission found that the overwhelming majority of victims of gross violations of human rights—killing, torture, abduction and severe ill treatment—during the apartheid years (at the hands of both the government and its opponents) were males. Testimony received by the Commission suggests that the number of men who died was six times that of women. Non-fatal gross violations of rights were inflicted on more than twice the number of men as women. Nor can the Commission be accused of having ignored women and their testimony. The majority of the Commission's deponents (55.3%) were female, and so sensitive was the Commission to the relatively small proportion of women amongst the victims of the most severe violations that it held a special hearing on women.

In the Kosovo conflict of 1998–1989, according to one study, 90% of the war-related deaths were of men, and men constituted 96% of people reported missing. According to the report of the Organization of Security and Co-operation in Europe (OSCE) Kosovo Verification Mission, "young men were the group that was by far the most targeted in the conflict in Kosovo." While women and girls constituted the majority of rape victims, men and boys were tortured and killed in much greater numbers.

These are but a few recent examples, in the long history of human violence, in which males have been the primary victims of mass murder and other serious human rights violations.

Periodical and Internet Sources Bibliography

The following articles have been selected to supplement the diverse views presented in this chapter.

Chaitra Arjunpuri   "'Honour Killings' Bring Dishonour to India," Al Jazeera, December 27, 2012. www.aljazeera .com.

David Benatar   "Let's Not Forget That Most Victims of Violent Crime Are Men, Not Women," *Cape Times* (Cape Town, South Africa), January 11, 2012.

Phyllis Chesler   "Worldwide Trends in Honor Killings," *Middle East Quarterly*, Spring 2010.

Nadia Shira Cohen   "Blood Feuds Still Boiling in Albania," *USA Today*, July 30, 2012.

Palash R. Ghosh   "Honor Killings: An Ancient Ritual," *International Business Times*, January 30, 2012.

Adam Jones   "Case Study: The Anfal Campaign (Iraqi Kurdistan), 1988," Gendercide Watch, n.d. www.gendercide.org.

Adam Jones   "Rape in the Military: An Open Letter to Kirby Dick," *Gendercide in the News* (blog), February 7, 2013. http://gendercidewatch.blogspot.com.

Melanie Judge   "Attention to Violence Must Challenge Masculinity, Not Entrench It," *Queery* (blog), February 14, 2012. http://queery.oia.co.za.

United Nations Population Fund   "Ending Widespread Violence Against Women," n.d. www.unfpa.org.

Bruce Watson   "A Hidden Crime: Domestic Violence Against Men Is a Growing Problem," DailyFinance, January 30, 2010. www.dailyfinance.com.

For Further Discussion

Chapter 1

1. Edgar Dahl suggests using sex-selection technology to ensure the births of sons. Does this seem like an ethical solution? Does it seem like it will address the broad problem of violence against women in India and China? Explain your answers, referring to other viewpoints in this chapter.

2. Based on the viewpoint by Susan Tiefenbrun and Christie J. Edwards and the viewpoint by Zbigniew Dumienski, do you believe that sex-selective abortion has contributed to sex trafficking in China? Would sex-selective abortion be ethical if it did *not* contribute to sex trafficking? Explain your answers.

Chapter 2

1. Does Keith Fournier oppose abortion in all cases, or just sex-selective abortion? Does this strengthen or weaken his position? Consider the other viewpoints in this chapter in your reply.

2. Heather Mallick says that the skewed ratio of boys to girls for third children among Indian immigrants "may mean something wildly other than what it seems." Does she offer any explanation as to what it might mean? Based on your readings in the first two chapters, what do you think the unbalanced sex ratio probably means?

Chapter 3

1. Heather McRobie and Rita Banerji define gendercide differently in relation to genocide. Which definition do you think is more accurate or useful? Explain your reasoning.

2. By Anthony Marino's reasoning, could the rape of men in wartime as discussed by Will Storr qualify as genocide?

Why or why not? Is it important to label mass rape as genocide? Again, why or why not?

Chapter 4

1. Do you think Alexander Christie-Miller would say that blood feuds in the Balkans are linked to the region's culture? Why or why not?

2. On the basis of the viewpoints by Sandra I. Cheldelin and David Benatar, do you believe that men or women experience worse gendercidal violence during war? Is this even a useful question to ask? Why or why not?

Organizations to Contact

The editors have compiled the following list of organizations concerned with the issues debated in this book. The descriptions are derived from materials provided by the organizations. All have publications or information available for interested readers. The list was compiled on the date of publication of the present volume; the information provided here may change. Be aware that many organizations take several weeks or longer to respond to inquiries, so allow as much time as possible.

Alan Guttmacher Institute

125 Maiden Lane, 7th Floor, New York, NY   10038

(212) 248-1111; toll-free: (800) 355-0244 • fax: (212) 248-1951

email: info@guttmacher.org

website: www.guttmacher.org

The institute is a sex and reproductive health research group. It uses statistical data and research to protect and expand the reproductive choices for men and women, including birth control and safe and legal abortion. Its publications include the annual *Perspectives on Sexual and Reproductive Health* and *International Perspectives on Sexual and Reproductive Health*, and *Guttmacher Policy Review*.

All Girls Allowed

101 Huntington Ave., Suite 2205, Boston, MA   02199

(617) 492-9099, ext. 236

website: www.allgirlsallowed.org

All Girls Allowed is a Christian organization that works to expose the injustice of China's one-child policy, to rescue girls and mothers from gendercide, and to celebrate women. Its website includes information on the one-child policy and gendercide, press releases, links, and other information.

Amnesty International
5 Penn Plaza, 14th Floor, New York, NY   10001
(212) 807-8400 • fax: (212) 463-9193
email: aimember@aiusa.org
website: www.amnestyusa.org

Amnesty International is a worldwide movement of people who campaign for internationally recognized human rights. Its vision is of a world in which every person enjoys all of the human rights enshrined in the Universal Declaration of Human Rights and other international human rights standards. Each year it publishes a report on its work and its concerns throughout the world. Amnesty International highlights gender-related violence and genocide as a human rights abuse in many articles and reports available through its website, such as "Bosnia and Herzegovina: Time for Republika Srpska to Make Reparations for Wartime Rape," and "Global Campaign Targets Rape in Conflict Zones."

Centre to End All Sexual Exploitation (CEASE)
PO Box 11471, Edmonton, AB   T59 3K6
  Canada
(780) 471-6143 • fax: (780) 471-6237
email: director@ceasenow.org
website: www.ceasenow.org

CEASE works to address sexual exploitation and the harms created by prostitution through public education, client support, counseling, and emergency poverty relief for individuals recovering from trauma and exploitation. Its website includes reports and articles on the effects of sexual exploitation and trafficking.

Gendercide Watch
email: gendercide_watch@hotmail.com
website: www.gendercide.org

Gendercide Watch seeks to confront acts of gender-selective mass killing around the world. It raises awareness, conducts research, and produces educational resources on gendercide.

Its main means of outreach and public education is its website, which includes a database of case studies and other research materials on gendercide. It also manages a moderated mailing list and maintains contacts and affiliations with scholars, students, and activists.

Genocide Intervention Network (GI-Net)

1025 Connecticut Ave. NW, Suite 310, Washington, DC 20036
(202) 599-7405 • fax: (202) 559-7410
email: info@genocideintervention.net
website: www.genocideintervention.net

GI-Net envisions a world in which the global community is willing and able to protect civilians from genocide and mass atrocities. In order to empower individuals and communities with the tools to prevent and stop genocide, GI-Net recommends activities from engaging government representatives to hosting fund-raisers. While maintaining many documents online regarding genocide, GI-Net provides an action plan to promote action as well as education.

Human Life International

4 Family Life Lane, Front Royal, VA 22630
(800) 549-5433 • fax: (540) 622-6247
email: hli@hli.org
website: www.hli.org

Human Life International is a Roman Catholic organization working worldwide to oppose what it considers the culture of death, including abortion, contraception, and euthanasia. It lobbies lawmakers, opposes pro-choice organizations, and works with pro-life advocates internationally. Publications available on its website include "The Case Against Condoms," and "Pro-life Talking Points."

Human Rights Watch (HRW)

350 Fifth Ave., 34th Floor, New York, NY 10118-3299
(212) 290-4700 • fax: (212) 736-1300

email: hrwnyc@hrw.org
website: www.hrw.org

Founded in 1978, this nongovernmental organization conducts systematic investigations of human rights abuses in countries around the world. It highlights sexual violence as a human rights abuse, during both peacetime and in conflict situations. HRW publishes many books and reports on specific countries and issues as well as annual reports, and other articles on gender violence and genocide.

Institute for the Study of Genocide (ISG)

John Jay College of Criminal Justice, New York, NY   10019
email: info@instituteforthestudyofgenocide.org
website: www.instituteforthestudyofgenocide.org

The ISG is an independent nonprofit organization that exists to promote and disseminate scholarship and policy analyses on the causes, consequences, and prevention of genocide. To attain these ends, it publishes a semiannual newsletter and working papers and holds periodic conferences; maintains liaisons with academic, human rights, and refugee organizations; provides consultation to representatives of media, governmental, and nongovernmental organizations; and advocates passage of legislation and administrative measures related to genocide and gross violations of human rights. In addition to newsletters, the ISG publishes books on the topic of genocide, such as *Ever Again? Evaluating the United Nations Genocide Convention on Its 50th Anniversary and Proposals to Activate the Convention.*

Physicians for Human Rights (PHR)

1156 Fifteenth Street NW, Suite 1001, Washington, DC   20005
(202) 728-5335 • fax: (202) 728-3053
website: http://physiciansforhumanrights.org

PHR is an independent organization that uses medicine and science to stop mass atrocities and human rights violations against individuals. It uses its investigations and expertise to advocate for the protection of human rights victims and the prosecution of those who violate human rights. One of the issues PHR focuses on is rape in wartime, and its website includes background information and reports, such as "The Use of Rape as a Weapon of War in Darfur, Sudan," and "Hidden Deaths of Libyan Rape Survivors."

Prevent Genocide International (PGI)
1804 S Street NW, Washington, DC   20009
(202) 483-1948 • fax: (202) 328-0627
email: info@preventgenocide.org
website: www.preventgenocide.org

PGI is a global education and action network established in 1998 with the purpose of bringing about the elimination of the crime of genocide. In an effort to promote education on the subject of genocide, PGI maintains a multilingual website both for the education of the international community as well as for the nations not yet belonging to the United Nations Genocide Convention in an effort to persuade these holdout countries join. Its website maintains a database of government documents and news releases, as well as original content provided by members.

Bibliography of Books

Beverly Allen   *Rape Warfare: The Hidden Genocide in Bosnia-Herzegovina and Croatia.* Minneapolis: University of Minnesota Press, 1996.

Debra B. Bergoffen   *Contesting the Politics of Genocidal Rape: Affirming the Dignity of the Vulnerable Body.* New York: Routledge, 2012.

Donald Bloxham and A. Dirk Moses   *The Oxford Handbook of Genocide Studies.* New York: Oxford University Press, 2010.

James Garrow   *The Pink Pagoda: One Man's Quest to End Gendercide in China.* Washington, DC: WND Books, 2012.

Susan Greenhaigh   *Just One Child: Science and Policy in Deng's China.* Berkeley: University of California Press, 2008.

Sonja M. Hedgepeth and Rochelle G. Saidel, eds.   *Sexual Violence Against Jewish Women During the Holocaust.* Waltham, MA: Brandeis University Press, 2010.

Dagmar Herzog, ed.   *Brutality and Desire: War and Sexuality in Europe's Twentieth Century.* New York: Palgrave Macmillan, 2009.

Georgina Holmes   *Women and War in Rwanda: Gender, Media and the Representation of Genocide.* London: I.B. Tauris, 2013.

Hua-Lun Huang   *The Missing Girls and Women of China, Hong Kong and Taiwan: A Sociological Study of Infanticide, Forced Prostitution, Political Imprisonment, "Ghost Brides," Runaways and Thrownaways, 1900–2000s.* Jefferson, NC: McFarland, 2012.

Mara Hvistendahl   *Unnatural Selection: Choosing Boys over Girls, and the Consequences of a World Full of Men.* Philadelphia: PublicAffairs Books, 2011.

Adam Jones   *Gender Inclusive: Essays on Violence, Men, and Feminist International Relations.* New York: Routledge, 2009.

Adam Jones, ed.   *Gendercide and Genocide.* Nashville: Vanderbilt University Press, 2004.

Christopher Kaczor   *The Ethics of Abortion: Women's Rights, Human Life, and the Question of Justice.* New York: Routledge, 2011.

Kamala Kempaddo, Jyoti Sanghera, and Bandana Pattanaik, eds.   *Trafficking and Prostitution Reconsidered: New Perspectives on Migration, Sex Work, and Human Rights.* 2nd ed. Boulder, CO: Paradigm, 2011.

D.E. Mugello   *Drowning Girls in China.* Lanham, MD: Rowman & Littlefield, 2008.

Tuisi Patel, ed.   *Sex-Selective Abortion in India.* Thousand Oaks, CA: Sage, 2006.

Nicole Pope   *Honor Killings in the Twenty-First Century.* New York: Palgrave Macmillan, 2012.

John K. Roth and   *Rape: Weapon of War and Genocide.*
Carol Rittner   St. Paul, MN: Paragon House, 2012.

Paul Schliesmann   *Honour on Trial: The Shafia Murders and the Culture of Honour Killings.* Markham, ON: Fitzhenry & Whiteside, 2013.

Louise Shelley   *Human Trafficking: A Global Perspective.* New York: Cambridge University Press, 2010.

Andrea Smith   *Conquest: Sexual Violence and American Indian Genocide.* Boston: South End, 2005.

Jane Springer   *Genocide.* Berkeley, CA: Groundwork Books, 2006.

Mary Anne   *Gendercide.* Totowa, NJ: Rowman and
Warren   Allanheld, 1985.

Hilmi M. Zawati   *The Triumph of Ethnic Hatred and the Failure of International Political Will: Gendered Violence and Genocide in the Former Yugoslavia and Rwanda.* Lewiston, NY: Edwin Mellen, 2010.

Index

A

Abortion
  anti-abortion movements, 84–97, 99–102
  British abortion law, 84–92
  by ethnicity 2011, 78*t*
  pregnancy counseling, 86–91
  See also Sex selection; Sex-selective abortion; Specific countries
Agduk, Meltem, 162
Albania, 173–179
Ali, Chomir, 168
All-China Women's Federation (ACWF), 40
Allen, Beverly, 131, 139
Alola Foundation, 67
Amnesty International, 114–115, 117
Anderson, S., 37
Anderson, Scott, 178
Andreas, P., 63
Apartheid, 120, 197
Armenia, 73, 190
ASEAN (Association of Southeast Asian Nations), 70
Asia Foundation, 40
Askin, Kelly, 132
Association of Concentration Camp Torture Survivors of Canton Sarajevo, 183
Association of Southeast Asian Nations (ASEAN), 62, 70
Atim, Salome, 147, 148

Atlantic Monthly (magazine), 18
Azerbaijan, 73

B

Baby hatches, 18
Banerji, Rita, 122–126
Bangkok Declaration on Irregular Migration (1999), 62
Bangladesh, 114, 168, 190
Bare Branches: The Security Implications of Asia's Surplus Male Population (Hudson and den Boer), 102
"Bare branches" (unmarried men) in China, 22, 28, 30, 53
Beese, Karin, 32–41
Begum, Manna, 168
Benatar, David, 194–198
Bindel, Julie, 158
Blood feuds. *See* Honor killings and blood feuds
Boehm, Christopher, 174–175
Book of Odes (Shijing), 29
Bosnia-Herzegovina, 117–118, 121, 127–141, 182–183, 185, 190–191
Bossen, Laurel, 34
Bowcott, Owen, 177, 179
Bristow, Jennie, 84–91
British Pregnancy Advisory Service (BPAS), 85
Brownmiller, Susan, 184
Bulte, E., 36

C

Canada, 104–113, 158
Canada Health Act, 106
Canadian Medical Association Journal, 109
Canadian Medical Journal, 105–107
CBC News, 107
Çetta, Anton, 179
Chang, Iris, 191, 192
Charny, Israel, 125
Cheldelin, Sandra I., 180–193
Child abandonment, 18, 44
Child brides, 53
China
    "bare branches" (unmarried men), 22, 28, 30, 53
    female status, 14, 24–25, 33–35, 39, 56
    health care, 15
    human rights, 24
    human trafficking, 52
    infanticide, 29, 36
    male status, 31, 33–34
    missing women, 37–38, 45, 56
    Nanjing massacre, 191–193
    purchase of brides, 52
    sex ratio of live births, 22, 23*t,* 28, 33, 35-38, 39*t,* 47
    sex-selective abortion, 21-24, 23*t,* 32–41, 93
    suicide and gender, 14
China's one-child policy (OCP)
    abortion of female fetuses, 32–41, 36
    development, 34–35
    enforcement, 35, 36, 38
    female depression and, 15
    infanticide and, 36

    missing women and, 37–38, 51, 56
    sex ratio of live births, 23–25, 33, 35–38
Christian Science Monitor (newspaper), 177
Christie-Miller, Alexander, 160–166
Chung, Woojin, 108
Clinton, Bill, 21–22
Clinton, Hillary, 48, 151
Colombia, 191
Confucius, 33
Congo, 144, 145, 183, 185–187, 197
Conquest, Robert, 197
Convention for the Suppression of White Slave Traffic (1910), 60
Convention on the Elimination of All Forms of Discrimination against Women (CEDAW), 49
Courtwright, David T., 28
Cradle baby schemes, 44
Cummings, Brian, 170

D

Daily Beast (website), 15
Daily Telegraph (newspaper), 85–88
Das Gupta, Monica, 30–31, 103
Davies, N., 60
Democratic Republic of the Congo (DRC), 144, 145, 183, 185–187, 197
Democratic Republic of Timor (East Timor), 59, 66, 191
Den Boer, Andrea M., 102
Deng, Aluel Mangong, 182
Desai, Kishwar, 75–83

Deutsche Press-Agentur
(newspaper), 179
Dice, Kay, 169
Dickson, Brian, 106
Doezema, Joe, 58
Dolan, Chris, 145, 149–150, 151
Domestic abuse, 14, 162, 195–196
Donnelly, Ciáran, 187
Dorries, Nadine, 85–86, 88, 89
Dowry tradition, 28, 30, 44–45,
    80–81, 124
Drost, Peter, 125
Dumienski, Zbigniew, 57–70
Dutch Oxfam, 150
Dworkin, Andrea, 159

E

East Timor (Democratic Republic
of Timor), 59, 66, 191
École Polytechnique at University
of Montreal, 158
The Economist (magazine), 20–25,
    27, 111
Edwards, Christie J., 50–56
Edwards, T., 33
El Salvador, 144
Engle, Karen, 130, 131–132
Equal rights, 38
Erdogan, Tayyip, 161–166
Ethnic cleansing, 134–136, 138–
    139

F

Family name, 34, 44, 73
Fan, Maureen, 14
Females
    abandonment, 36, 44
    blood feud immunity, 174–
        176
    child brides, 53
    depression, 15
    domestic abuse, 14, 162
    dowry tradition, 28, 30, 44–
        45, 80–81, 124
    education, 24–25, 39, 43–44,
        48, 166
    employment, 44
    as financial liability, 18–19, 34,
        44–45, 78–80
    government assistance, 39, 49
    honor killings and, 161–166
    infanticide, 27–29, 36
    Japanese "comfort women",
        189–190
    missing girls/women, 37–38,
        45–46, 48, 51, 56, 76–77, 80,
        97, 102
    property inheritance, 24–25
    purchase of brides, 52
    sale of infant girls, 53
    sex selection of babies, 20–25,
        23, 31, 36
    status in society, 14, 15, 24–
        25, 28, 33–35, 39, 48, 56, 115
    suicide, 14–16, 55
    "sworn virgins", 175–176
    War on Women, 95, 95n2
    See also Human trafficking;
        Prostitution; Sex crimes; Sex
        ratio of live births; War;
        Specific countries
Femicide, 119
Field, Frank, 86, 88
Firat, Hatice, 163, 166
Fisher, Siobhán K., 132
Forbes (magazine), 114
Forced labor, 51–52, 59–61, 63
Fortune (magazine), 96
Fournier, Keith, 92–97

G

Gandhi, Indira, 79
Gender Against Men
  (documentary), 149
Gender apartheid, 120
Gendercide
  definition, 117
  as genocide, 116–126
  Guatemala, 117–119
  honor killings, 160–166
  infanticide, 18, 27–28, 29, 36,
    102
  male gendercide, 114, 194–198
  Mexico, 117–120
  minimizing, 120
  See also Females; Males; Sex
    selection; Sex-selective abor-
    tion
*Gendercide: Sex Selection in
  America* (documentary), 99–100
Gendercide Watch (website), 18,
  114, 158, 190
Genocide
  definition, 117
  ethnic cleansing, 134–136,
    138–139
  gendercide as, 116–126
  India, 123–126, 190
  sex crimes as, 127–141
  See also Gendercide; Infanti-
    cide; Sex selection; Sex-
    selective abortion; Specific
    countries
Georgia, 73
Germany, 152–157, 189, 190, 192
Ghorbani-Zarin, Arash, 168
Goldberg, Michelle, 98–103
Goodwin, Jan, 185
Gorji, Hafija, 170–171
Grant, Linda, 117–118

Greenhill, K., 63
The Guardian (newspaper), 16,
  158, 176, 177, 183
Guatemala, 117–119
Gullu, Cana, 162

H

Haqverdi, Aliya, 73
Hasija, Namrata, 15–16
Hentoff, Nat, 181, 182, 184
Herzegovina (Bosnia-
  Herzegovina), 117–118, 121,
  127–141, 182–183, 185, 190
Hinduism, 28
Holocaust, 152–157, 190
Homosexuality, 170
Honor killings and blood feuds
  Balkans, 172–179
  Committee of Blood Recon-
    ciliation, 177, 179
  female immunity in blood
    feuds, 174-176
  females kills, 161-166
  Pakistan, 176
  Turkey, 160-166, 164-165*t*
  United Kingdom, 167–171
Hossain, Anushay, 114
Hovhannisyan, Parandzem, 73
Hoxha, Enver, 176
Hrdy, Sarah Blaffer, 28
Hu Jintao, 24
Hudson, Valerie M., 102
Huffington Post (website), 104–107
Human Fertilization and Embry-
  ology Authority (UK), 77
Human Rights Watch (HRW),
  170, 186

Human trafficking
black market trade of infants, 55
definition, 52, 59
foreign adoption, 55
historically, 59–60
international trafficking, 52–55
as myth, 57–70
poverty, 52
"rescue industry," 65–66
scarcity of women and, 46–47, 51
sex trafficking as gendercide, 50–56
statistics, 58
US Department of State Trafficking in Persons (TIP) Report, 51, 61, 63
Hutus, 183–184, 185

I

Ibrahim, Hisamuddin, 171
Ibrahim, Mo, 170–171
ICTY (International Criminal Tribunal for Yugoslavia), 133
India
baby hatches, 18
dowry tradition, 28, 30, 44–45, 80–81, 124
education of females, 43–44
employment rates for women, 44
female children as liability, 18–19, 44–45, 78–80
genocide, 123–126
girls age 0 to 6 years 1961–2011, *124*
infanticide, 18, 27–28, 123
Kashmir/Punjab/Delhi massacre, 190

legislation against sex selection, 31
male children as asset, 18–19, 31, 78–80
missing women, 37–38, 45–46, 48, 76, 80
religion, 28, 31
sex ratio of live births, 22, 43–44, 80
sex-selective abortion, 21–22, 21–24, 42–49, 75–83, 93, 123
virginity, 81
Infanticide
China, 29, 36, 56
definition, 27
as genocide, 126
India, 18–19, 27–28, 123
missing women and, 102
prevalence, 102
Mary Anne Warren on, 190
as worst crime, 27
Institute for War and Peace Reporting, 73
Institute of Peace and Conflict Studies, 14, 15
Intelligender Gender Prediction Test, 96
International Agreement for the Suppression of the White Slave Traffic (1904), 60
International Convention for the Suppression of the Traffic in Women and Children (1921), 60
International Convention for the Suppression of the Traffic in Women of Full Age (1913), 60
International Court of Justice (ICJ), 129, 133, 140
International Labour Organization (ILO), 61

International Rescue Committee (IRC), 187
International Women's Day, 161
IOM (International Organization for Migration), 68
Iqbal, Habib, 171
Iraq, 170
Iron Curtain, 60

J

Japan, 30, 189, 189–193
Jews, 124, 126, 132, 153–157, 190
Jhareja Rajputs, 27–28
Jolis, Branko, 176
Jones, Adam, 18, 114, 158, 172
Jordan, Michael J., 177
Journal of the American Medical Association, 148, 186

K

Kainth, Gursharan Singh, 42–49
Kakuk, Gyorgy, 68
Kale, Rajendar, 105–107
Kanat, Gulsun, 163
Karadzic, Radovan, 117, 120, 121
Kashmir/Punjab/Delhi massacre, 190
Khan, Irene, 114–115
Koch, Tom, 109–110
Kosovo, 173–175, 179, 198
Kunarac, Dragoljub, 133–134
Kunarac, Prosecutor v., 133

L

Lamthi, Shtjefen, 178
Lansley, Andrew, 85, 87, 88–90
Lépine, Marc, 158–159

Li Ke-hen, 192
Li Weixiong, 54
LifeSiteNews (website), 73–74
Liisanantti, Anu, 32–41
Live Action, 95, 97, 102
Lui Qian, 40

M

MacArthur, Douglas, 190
MacKinnon, Catharine, 132
Makerere University's Refugee Law Project (RLP), 143
Malcolm, Noel, 173–174
Male Rape and Human Rights (Stemple), 144
Males
  "bare branches" (unmarried men) in China, 22, 28, 30, 53
  domestic abuse, 14, 162
  family name, 34, 44, 73
  gendercide, 114, 194–198
  honor killings, 167–171
  missing males, 177
  parental care, 73
  property inheritance, 24–25, 33–34, 44, 82
  rape of males, 142–151, 196
  Stalin purges, 197
  suicide, 15
  value in society, 28, 44, 78–80
  as violent crime victims, 196–198
Mallick, Heather, 108–113
Mangal, Feroz, 169
Mao Zedong, 25, 34–35
Marino, Anthony, 127–141
McGreal, Chris, 183, 184
McRobie, Heather, 116
Mei-Hua, 16

Mekshi, Gjin, 177, 179
Men. *See* Males
Mexico, 117–120
Miah, Mohammed, 171
Miah, Sadek, 171
MicroSort, 31
Military Tribunal of the Far East, 193
Miller, Heidi, 14–15
Milton, Anne, 86, 89
Misogyny, 99, 100, 121, 158
Missing people
  China's missing women, 37–38, 45, 51, 56
  India's missing women, 37–38, 45–46, 48, 76, 80
  missing males, 177
  sex selection and, 37–38, 44–46, 48, 51, 56, 76–77, 80, 97, 102
Mladic, Ratko, 121
Mohammed, Abdullah, 171
Mohammed, Aysha, 171
Mohanty, Ranjani Iyer, 18
Morgentaler, R. v., 106
Mother Nature (Hrdy), 28
Muslims, 127–141, 132, 160–171, 181–182

N

Nanjing Military Tribunal for the Trial of War Criminals, 193
The Nation (magazine), 185
National Academy of Sciences (NAS), 96
NBC, 184
New York Post (newspaper), 184
New York Times (newspaper), 115, 176

New York Times Magazine, 178
Newsweek (magazine), 184
North Korea, 63
Ntinda, Angella, 148

O

Organization of Security and Co-operation in Europe (OSCE)
  Kosovo Verification Mission, 198
Owiny, Eunice, 143, 145, 150

P

Pakistan, 114, 176, 184
Parliamentary Assembly of the Council of Europe (PACE), 73
Pelletier, Francine, 158
Pesticides, 15–16
Pinto, Freida, 79
Pipes, Daniel, 167–171
Planned Parenthood, 95, 97, 99
Population and Family Planning Association (PFPAC), 40
Poverty and wealth, 14, 15, 23, 24, 45, 52, 77, 103
Pregnancy counseling, 86–91
Prenatal Nondiscrimination Act (PRENDA), 93, 97, 101
Property inheritance, 24–25, 33–34, 44, 82
Prosecutor v. Kunarac, 133
Prostitution
  forced prostitution, 52, 54, 56, 59, 137, 154, 189–190
  high sex-ratio societies and, 55
  human trafficking, 51, 62
  US soldiers and, 189–190

Protocol to Prevent Suppress and Punish Trafficking in Persons, Especially Women and Children, 61
Psychosocial Recovery and Development in East Timor (PRADET), 68

R

R. v. Morgentaler, 106
Rahman, Mamnoor, 168
Rahman, Mohammed Mujibar, 168
Rahman, Sheikh Mujibur, 114
Rai, Aishwarya, 79
Ramgaj, Perlat, 179
Rape of Nanking (Chang), 191
Rape of Nanking (Yin and Young), 191–192
Rape Warfare: The Hidden Genocide in Bosnia-Herzegovina and Croatia (Allen), 131
Rapes in Bosnia-Herzegovina (Stiglmayer), 129
Ray, D., 37
Refugee Law Project (RLP) of Makerere University, 143
Religion
female status in society and, 28
  Hinduism, 28
  Islam (Muslims), 127–141, 132, 160–171, 181–182
  Judaism (Jews), 124, 126, 132, 153–157
  male status in society and, 33–34
  sex selection and, 28, 31, 44
"Rescue industry," 65–66
Rodina, Mihaela, 177

Rose, Lila, 95, 97
Roy, Nilanjana S., 115
Rrushkadoli, Leka, 178
Rummell, R.J., 114
Russell, Diana, 126
Rwanda, 185, 190

S

Sadiqi, Hasibullah, 169
Sadiqi, Khatera, 169
Saidel, Rochelle, 152–157
Sen, Amartya, 22, 33, 102
Serbia, 128
Sex crimes
  Bangladesh, 114–115
  as ethnic cleansing, 134–136, 139
  forced impregnation, 131–136, 140
  as genocide, 127–141
  Holocaust, 153–155
  Japanese "comfort women," 189–190
  male rapes, 142–151, 195
  ostracism by community and, 114
  percentage of conflicts with reported rape 1990–2009, *188*
  revenge rape, 187–189
  state sanctioned, 190
  suicide, 114
  US soldiers and, 189–190
  as war crime, 137
  as war weapon, 117–118, 144, 180–193
Sex industry, 62, 64, 67, 69
See also Prostitution

Sex ratio of live births
China, 22, 23*t*, 28, 33, 35-38, 39*t*, 47
human trafficking and, 55
India, 22, 43–44, 80
negative effects of unbalanced ratio, 22
second-order births, 38
US ratios 2013, 101*t*
wealth and poverty and, 23, 45
Sex Ratios by Birth Order in China 2005, 39*t*
Sex selection
infanticide, 27–28
legislation against sex selection, 31
marriage prospects for men and, 22, 28, 30, 46–47
missing women and, 37–38, 44–46, 48, 51, 56, 76–77, 80, 97, 102
religious beliefs and, 28, 31
United States, 102–103
wealth and poverty and, 23, 24, 45, 77, 103
Sex-selective abortion
anti-abortion movements and, 84–97, 99–103
China, 21-24, 23*t*, 32–41, 40, 93
European countries, 73
immigrant women, 105
India, 21–24, 42–49, 75–83, 93, 123
punishment for doctors, 101
status of females and, 24–25, 39–40
theory for reduction of, 98–103
ultrasounds, 21, 23, 36–37, 46, 48, 76, 104–113
wealth and poverty and, 23, 24, 77

Sexual Violence Against Jewish Women During the Holocaust (Hedgepeth and Saidel), 135
Sexually transmitted diseases, 190
Shank, Megan, 15
Shetty, Shilpa, 79
Singapore, 22, 23
Slavery, 51–52, 59–61, 63
Society of Obstetricians and Gynecologists of Canada, 107
South Africa, 120, 185, 197–198
South Korea, 22, 24, 103
Srebrenica, Bosnia, 117–118, 190–191
Sri Lanka, 144
Stalin, Joseph, 189, 190, 197
Stemple, Lara, 144, 149, 150–151
Stiglmayer, Alexandra, 129
Stockholm Syndrome, 66, 66n1
Storr, Will, 142–151
Strauss, Julius, 176
Stump, Doris, 73–74
Sudan, 181–182
Suicide, 14, 15, 55, 83, 114
Sweden, 73
"Sworn virgins," 175–176

T

Taiwan, 22, 23, 52
Tesanovic, Jasmine, 182–183
Thailand, 52
Tiefenbrun, Susan, 33, 50–56
Tito, Marshall Josip Broz, 128, 128n1, 176
Toronto Star (newspaper), 109–110
Trafficking. *See* Human trafficking
Trivers, Robert, 30
Trotta, Liz, 184
Truth and Reconciliation Commission of South Africa, 197–198

Turkey, 161–166
Turkish Association of Women's Federations, 162

U

Uganda, 143–151
Ultrasounds, 21, 23, 36–37, 46, 48, 76, 104–113
UN Convention against Transnational Organized Crime, 61
UN Convention on the Prevention and Punishment of the Crime of Genocide (CPPCG), 123, 133
UN Final Report of the Commission of Experts, 137, 138
UN Office for the Coordination of Humanitarian Affairs (OCHA), 185
UN Security Council Resolution 1325, 151
UN Trafficking Protocol, 82
UNHCR (UN High Commission for Refugees), 150
US Department of State Trafficking in Persons (TIP) Report, 51, 61, 63
US sex ratio of live births, 2013, 101*t*

V

Value Land: Single Men and Social Disorder from the Frontier to the Inner City (Courtwright), 28
Van Woudenberg, Anneke, 186
Vietnam, 185
Village Voice (newspaper), 181

Violent crime, 196–198
   See also Honor killings and blood feuds; Sex crimes; War
Virginity, 81

W

Wallström, Margot, 150
War
   Nanjing massacre, 191–193
   sex crimes, 117–118, 137, 142–151, 180–193
   "on women," 95, 95n2
   war trials, 129, 133, 140
   See also Specific countries
"War on women," 95, 95n2
Warren, Mary Anne, 190
Washington Post (newspaper), 14
Wealth and poverty, 14, 15, 23, 24, 45, 52, 77, 103
White, Hilary, 73–74
Willard, Dan, 30
Women in Berlin: Eight Weeks in the Conquered City (Anonymous), 187–189
Women of 1971 (Brownmiller), 184
World Bank, 103
World Economic Forum's Global Gender Gap, 165
World Health Organization (WHO), 14

Y

Yag, Gulhan, 161, 163, 166
Yildirim, Arzu, 162
Yin, James, 191–192
Yirmibesoglu, Vildan, 166
Young, Shi, 191–192
Yugoslavia, 128n1, 129